WHAT'S YOUR QUESTION?

What's Your Question?

by
KEN SUMRALL

WHITAKER BOOKS · 1972

© Whitaker Books—1972
All rights reserved
First Printing—20,000 Copies

Whitaker Books
607 Laurel Drive
Monroeville, Pennsylvania 15146

TABLE OF CONTENTS

	PREFACE	7
	INTRODUCTION	9
1.	ASTROLOGY, HOROSCOPES, HYPNOTISM	11
2.	CHRISTIANS AND THEIR PROBLEMS (conscience, gloominess, inferiority, religion)	17
3.	CHURCH PRACTICES AND BELIEFS (pleading the Blood, church attendance, dismissing pastors, evolution, fasting, raising hands, sabbath, tithe, women)	23
4.	DEMONS	33
5.	DENOMINATIONAL QUESTIONS (Why so many?)	39
6.	EMOTIONALISM AND GOD	45
7.	ETERNITY ISSUES (eternal security, heathen, Hell, predestination)	51
8.	COMMENTS, EXPLANATIONS (Anti-Christ, celibacy, reason, sinning preachers, snake handling, superstar opera, unforgivable sin)	57
9.	GLOSSALALIA (speaking in tongues)	67
10.	MIRACLES AND HEALING	93
11.	RACIAL ISSUES	99
12.	SEX AND THE BIBLE (abortion, birth control, homosexuality, sex education)	101
13.	"WORLDLY" ISSUES (dancing, jewelry, wigs)	107

PREFACE

It is a pleasure to preface this book for Brother Ken Sumrall. I first met Bro. Sumrall at the New Orleans Theological Seminary, where we were both enrolled. Through the years we have exchanged pulpits on numerous occasions and enjoyed fellowship. Our congregation in Mobile, the Bay View Heights Baptist Church, has always received his ministry enthusiastically and benefited greatly.

While the congregation has been greatly blessed by his ministry, my personal life has been profoundly affected. In 1962, when he preached his first series of meetings in Mobile I observed his personal devotional life. Having known many ministers, and being raised in the home of a Godly minister, I quickly recognized Bro. Ken had a special touch of God on his life. As Jacob, who limped after God touched his thigh, Bro. Ken bore a subdued awareness of God's sovereign power. Evidence of his devotional life was his knowledge of Scriptures. Literally, he could cite the reference to practically any New Testament quotation. I say this, not to flatter or embarrass my friend, but to substantiate my own personal respect for his ministry. This was Bro. Ken as I knew him in 1962.

In 1964 my own ministry seemed dry, fruitless and impudent. Several books, including the life story of Charles G. Finney, had fallen into my hands. Finney gave vivid testi-

Preface

mony to being baptized in the Holy Spirit, subsequent to his conversion. It was in March 1964 that God again brought Bro. Sumrall to my attention. A friend related to me how Bro. Sumrall had received the Baptism in the Holy Spirit. Had it been someone else, I might have dismissed the whole thing. However, Bro. Sumrall would entertain no experience that he had not studied Scripturally and thoroughly. After counseling with him, my feelings were confirmed. The study I had been making, Finney's testimony and other testimonies, pointed to the validity of this experience. It was a few weeks later that I received the Baptism in the Holy Spirit.

Now, several years later, many major news and communications media (Look, Life, Time, CBS, NBC, ABC) have acknowledged that something phenomenal is happening regarding the Holy Spirit. The amazing revival of interest in Jesus Christ, and the work of the Holy Spirit, is creating a dramatic need and desire for Bible teaching.

After reading the articles compiled here, I can say that they answer many of the common questions around the land today regarding the work of the Holy Spirit. These are practical articles. Bro. Sumrall is a very practical person and gives Scriptural answers. The Bible must be the final test of every philosophy, psychology and dogma.

These articles are taken from a series printed in the Pensacola News Journal. No attempt is made to select only the friendly questions, or the easy ones. These are questions that were asked by the kind of people we must reach with truth. Some are hostile, some are cynical, some are even humorous. In each case Bro. Ken attempts to squarely and Scripturally face the issue. You will not only benefit from these articles, you will also enjoy them.

Charles Simpson

WHAT IS YOUR QUESTION?
INTRODUCTION

In February, 1964, I was ushered into a new dimension of living by receiving the Baptism in the Holy Spirit with the evidence of speaking in "unknown" tongues. Prior to that time in thirteen years as a minister, I had committed to memory a large part of the Bible. The Spirit of God made the Word alive within me and brought me further into a teaching ministry in the Church, in home prayer groups, seminars, by radio, and newspaper. I began to receive questions from many places; many of these questions came from interested people in Pensacola, Florida, my home town. At that time it did not occur to me that my answers should be placed in print. However, in June, 1969, I began an article in the Sunday **Pensacola News Journal** entitled "What Is Your Question?" Readers were invited to send questions which they desired to be scripturally answered. The response has been beyond all my expectations. Many of the questions have been controversial; I have attempted to answer the questions with charity but with conviction.

I have been encouraged by many of my friends to print the newspaper articles in booklet form. Therefore, these questions and answers are published with the prayer that they will be profitable to those who have been confronted with the same questions by the curious, the spiritually hungry, and the gainsayers. They are presented here in the same simple form

Introduction

in which they appeared in the newspaper, with the exception of some effort made to compile questions of the same subject matter together for clarity.

Since these answers were written for the "common people," no effort has been made for scholarly presentation. My only desire is to present truth as simply and clearly as possible.

CHAPTER ONE

ASTROLOGY, HO ROSCOPES, HYPNOTISM

What do you think about reading horoscopes?

God has promised guidance to His people; but He condemns heathen practices of seeking guidance by meteors, planets, signs of Zodiac, magic arts, witchcraft, or in the name of astrology. These heathen practices include (1) enchantments or magical arts (Exodus 7:11; Leviticus 19:26; Acts 19:19); (2) witchcraft—practice of dealing with evil spirits (Deuteronomy 19:10; I Samuel 15:23; II Chronicles 33:6); (3) divination or fortune telling (Numbers 22:7; Acts 16:16); (4) necromancy or pretended communication with the dead (Deuteronomy 18:11; Isaiah 8:19; I Chronicles 10:13); (5) prognostication or to foretell by omens, signs, etc. (Isaiah 47:13); (6) astrology and star gazing (Jeremiah 10:2; Daniel 1:20).

All of these practices were and still are practiced in connection with demons or "familiar spirits." This includes horoscope readings.

For many years church theologians have denied the existence of demons. They have taught that Jesus' words about demons were nothing more than an attempt by Jesus to use the vocabulary of the times in explaining sicknesses and human traits or weaknesses. Therefore, most people have not

What's Your Question?

been taught the interest of demons in the affairs of people. In our day there is an awakening to the supernatural and the unseen spirit world. The results of this awakening are twofold. (1) Many are being made aware of the truth of God's Word concerning unseen demon forces and ways to combat them with the Word of God. They are seeking God's power; they are learning the truth of Satan's defeat at Calvary and how to resist Satanic forces through the Blood of Jesus Christ (Colossians 2:14-15; Ephesians 6:10-17; Revelation 12:10-11). They seek for guidance God's way (Psalms 119:105; John 16:13). (2) Others are being seduced by evil spirits into thinking that they are receiving guidance from God or science, when in reality they are receiving guidance and supernatural manifestations from "familiar spirits" under the direction of the god of this unbelieving world—Satan (II Corinthians 4:4).

It is not wrong to seek guidance from God, but I would seek no guidance which is contrary to the Bible.

What do you think of Jeane Dixon? Does her power to predict the future come from God?

Since Mrs. Dixon has so many followers, evidently a number of them in this Northwest Florida region, this is quite an explosive question. Fully realizing that some shall heap anathemas on my head for this answer, I unhesitatingly state that I do not believe Mrs. Dixon receives her powers from God, but from Satan.

Anyone who believes in the verbal inspiration and infallibility of the Bible can quickly discern the source of information that is obtained through the use of palm reading, crystal gazing, cards, vibrations, horoscopes, magic, etc. (Deuteronomy 18:9-12; 2 Chronicles 33:6; Galatians 5:19-21; Acts

Astrology, Horoscopes, Hypnotism

8:9–11; 16:16). All of these practices were and still are carried on in connection with demons called familiar spirits.

Mrs. Dixon makes no attempt to hide that she uses cards, crystal balls, palm reading, etc., to obtain her information. She believes in reincarnation and says that the spirit within her lived in another age in another person. This is probably true, since I believe her to be possessed by a familiar spirit which no doubt possessed someone else before the person's death.

The predictions of Mrs. Dixon have often come true, but this does not mean that God is the author of these predictions. Satan is the god of this world and has control of all those who have not made Jesus Christ Lord. He can cause chaos and can give the information of a tragedy in advance. He is FAMILIAR with many things, and it is an easy matter to convey information if he can find a "medium."

Of course, the most dangerous aspect of this woman's work is that she lives in Washington, D.C., and has a tremendous influence on many of our nation's leaders (Isaiah 47:13). Let us who believe what I am saying pray and bind these familiar spirits in the Name of Jesus (Matthew 18:18–20).

What is your opinion of Edgar Cayce? Do you believe in predicting the future through clairvoyance? Is this supernatural and of God?

Clairvoyance is to be classed with spiritualism, mediums, witches, and soothsayers, which the Bible condemns in no uncertain terms. Yes, it is supernatural but it is Satanic. There is a true "word of knowledge" ministry through the Holy Spirit (I Corinthians 12:8). But wherever there is the genuine gift of the Holy Spirit, Satan attempts to counterfeit

What's Your Question?

it (II Corinthians 11:13–15; II Thessalonians 2:9–12; Deuteronomy 13:1–3; Jeremiah 23:28–29; I John 4:1–3).

One great test of a "prophet" is whether he believes what the Holy Scripture says about sin (Romans 3:23), eternal hell (Matthew 5:29–30), the Blood of Jesus Christ (Hebrews 9:14, 22; I John 1:7–9), resurrection (John 5:25–29), the Second Coming of Christ (Acts 1:11, Revelation 1:7), and other fundamental Scriptures. If he does not believe these things, he is no true prophet of the God of the Bible.

These are not pleasant answers but Jesus warned of false prophets in sheep's clothing. Many wolves are traveling the land deceiving people through "familiar spirits" which the Bible warns us against (Leviticus 20:27; I Samuel 28:7, etc.).

There are two real dangers for people of this day. One is "gullibility" to accept everything supernatural as of God. The other is to classify everything supernatural as of the Devil (Mark 3:29). Acts 17:11 records a good attitude. "They received the word with all readiness of mind, and searched the Scriptures daily whether those things were so."

My minister is against hypnotism. How do you feel about it? Is it good or evil?

The word hypnotism comes from the Greek word "hypnos," meaning "sleep." Mr. Fraz A. Mesmer began experimenting in mind control in the 18th century and was able to induce abnormal concentration on any willing subject causing the subject to obey his suggestions. This was called mesmerism and was condemned by the medical and religious world of that day. The modern name was given to the act by an English physician named James Braid and has been brought into good repute by its usefulness in curbing pain during operations, childbirth, dental surgery, etc. It has also been used by some psychiatrists to analyze the past incidents

Astrology, Horoscopes, Hypnotism

of a person's life. Amazing feats have been accomplished through hypnotism. For example, one person under hypnosis was told that a red-hot iron would touch him. When the person was touched by a cold object, a blister rose on the spot. Another example is that a person was able to multiply 267 × 3,892 instantly in his head.

I believe hypnotism is in the realm of the supernatural and is the same as the black magic which is condemned in no uncertain terms by the Scriptures. An example may be found in Acts 8:9–11. The word "sorcery" here should be "magic." The control of your mind and your will power is given to you by God. To become simply passive and give your mind and will power into the hands of another human being is an open door for evil spirits. The hypnotist may be innocent, but remember, that even the best intentioned practitioner is only experimenting. It remains to be seen what the permanent results of hypnosis will be. The practice of hypnosis is to deceive, which we know to be the main device of the Devil.

Personally, I would never give the Devil a chance in my life by having my fortune told, consulting an astrologer, nor giving my mind over to a hypnotist. The Scriptures say: "Regard not them that have familiar spirits, neither seek after wizards to be defiled by them: I am the Lord your God" (Leviticus 19:31).

Dear Ken: You always manage to show your lack of knowledge. You should advise your people not to permit an amateur to hypnotize them. Under the skilled hands of a medical doctor, psychologist, or professional hypnotist, good results can be obtained such as operations, oral extractions, diseases eradicated, alcoholism cured, natural childbirth, etc. Before you print any more about what you don't know, why don't you get an authority on the subject? It may tire your weak mind. In a

What's Your Question?

former life (reincarnation) you were the man who set fire to people to be burned at the stake and you continue to persecute and hate in this life. God is love, but Ken Sumrall is hate. God even loves astrologers, fortune tellers, and card readers. Have fun in the lake of fire. You are condemning your soul as you condemn God's children.

I do not claim to be an expert in the field of hypnosis. I surely have no experimental knowledge of the subject and do not plan to have such. I have read enough on the subject to know that there are differences of opinion as to its use even among medical scientists (**Hypnosis and Suggestion,** by Dr. H. Bernheim). If you will notice, I mentioned some outstanding feats accomplished through hypnosis. However, even if the external signs are favorable, the damage done to the soul of man could be incalculable.

I say this in the light of the Word of God. Hypnosis is not new. It is as old as the heathen rites of the 15th century BC which the Bible condemns in no uncertain terms. For example, it was a common practice among idol worshippers to put people into a trance and cause them to walk through fire without evidence of any pain. But God said: "There shall not be found among you any one that maketh his son or daughter pass through the fire . . ." (Deuteronomy 18:10). The text classes the act with evil spirits.

Of course, you are entitled to your opinion. In fact, I am sure the **News Journal** will sell you space to express your brand of love, and your beliefs in reincarnation, spiritualism, etc. As for me, I was asked for my opinion and I gave it. Show me one alcoholic permanently cured by hypnosis and I'll show you many who have been cured through faith in the cleansing Blood of Jesus. While I respect true science, I believe that it is more important to heed "Thus saith the Lord" rather than "thus said Dr. So-and-so."

CHAPTER TWO

CHRISTIANS AND THEIR PROBLEMS

Dear Brother Sumrall . . . Here's one question you've probably been asked many times. How far should I go in letting my conscience be my guide in doing what is right and wrong?

The Bible says a lot about the conscience. For example, we are told that a person can have "a good conscience" (Acts 23:1); "a purged conscience" (Hebrews 9:9, 14; 10:2); "a weak conscience" (I Corinthians 8:7, 12, 13); "a pure conscience" (2 Timothy 1:3); "an evil conscience" (Hebrews 10:22); or "a seared conscience" (I Timothy 4:2).

The basic difference between man and animal is that animal has body and soul (Genesis 1:19) and man has body, soul, and spirit (Genesis 2:7). "The spirit of man is the lamp of the Lord" (Proverbs 20:27). The conscience is the inner voice of the spirit of man. It is through the conscience that God convicts a person of his sins (John 8:9) and the person can respond to God's call and be saved. The new birth takes place within the spirit of man when he receives Jesus Christ as his Lord and Saviour (John 3:1–16). "That which is born of the Spirit is spirit" (not body or soul). In simple words, Jesus plants His life within a man's spirit and purges his conscience with the Blood of the Cross (Hebrews 9:14).

However, the conscience can only become a good guide as it becomes Bible conscious. It must be trained in the Word by hiding the Word in the heart.

What's Your Question?

The reason why one Christian considers a thing wrong and another does not is the difference in consciences. Some have Baptist consciences; some have Methodist consciences; some have Pentecostal consciences; others have their own particular denominational consciences according to their training. God, hasten the day when we all have BIBLE-ORIENTED CONSCIENCES and become one in faith (Ephesians 4:13). Only then can we let our consciences be our guide.

I know I am saved through the Blood of the Lord Jesus Christ, but as hard as I try, I cannot live a joyful, victorious Christian life. Sometimes I am up, but most of the time I'm discouraged and down. Most everything I do turns into defeat. Please don't tell me to pray more for I have begged God day and night to help me. There seems to be no answer from God. I believe I love the Lord, but I can't seem to do anything right. What's wrong with me?

You have nothing wrong that cannot be solved by the truth. "Ye shall know the truth and the truth shall set you free" (John 8:32).

The words you wrote to me have the seed of defeat in them. For example, "As hard as I try . . . I cannot . . . most of the time I'm down . . . defeat . . . begged God . . . no answer . . . I can't . . ."

Multitudes of Christians are defeated because they talk defeat and failure. We can never rise above the level of our own words. If we talk defeat, fear, sickness, and unbelief, we will live that way. If we talk God's Word, we will live on that level. Therefore, learn to say what God says in His Word. Even when you pray, simply remind God of His Word. If God's people learn to meditate on the Word, they will have good success (Psalms 1:1-4).

My dear friend, remember that Satan is the accuser of the

brethren (Revelation 12:10–11). He desires your defeat and failure. He wants you to be anxious and worried, then you will be sick. Your words of defeat will cooperate with him. Proverbs 6:2, "Thou art snared by the words of thy mouth and thou art taken (captive) by the words of thy mouth."

Begin today to practice talking faith, not doubt. Jesus is the High Priest of your confession (Hebrews 3:1–2). You have what you say (Mark 11:22). Confess, then possess. Let me know how you make out.

How can I overcome an inferiority complex? I have been troubled with this all my life and cannot seem to get any victory over it. Is there something I can do to combat these terrible periods of depression that come because I feel so limited in most everything?

You did not say, but I assume that you have trusted the Lord Jesus Christ as your Lord and Saviour and have been "born again." If not, that is your first step (Romans 10:9, 10; John 3:1–16).

Your next step is to be filled with the Holy Ghost (Acts 1:4, 5; Acts 2:4; Acts 19:6; Ephesians 5:18). The Spirit of God will give you boldness and confidence. Contrast Peter's cowardice in Luke 22 and his boldness as portrayed in the Book of Acts. The Spirit of God made the difference.

If you still have difficulty in this area after you have taken these two steps, then remember that Christ lives in you. If you are a "Christ-container," then you are not inferior because there is nothing inferior about Christ. Without Christ we can do nothing (John 15:1–7). With Christ we can do all things (Philippians 4:13).

Since none of us can rise higher than our confession, begin to confess the Words of God concerning who you are and your victory in Christ.

What's Your Question?

For example, say, "I am a new creature in Christ" (2 Corinthians 5:17). "I am more than a conqueror in Christ" (Romans 8:37). "I will always triumph because Christ is in me" (2 Corinthians 2:14). "I can do all things through Christ who strengtheneth me" (Philippians 4:13). Repeat these verses and others like them until they become a part of you. You will sense yourself beginning to stand up inside. Do not say what you feel about yourself. Say what God says. His Word is TRUTH! The secret is not in yourself, but in God! "Not that we are sufficient of ourselves to think anything as of ourselves; but our sufficiency is of God" (2 Corinthians 3:5).

We have been able to help hundreds of people like yourself by these instructions. I confess now that you, also, will be helped (Job 22:28).

A psychiatrist has told a friend of mine who is receiving treatment for mental depression that "too much religion" is her trouble. He will not allow her to read a Bible or to attend church. Do you believe that a person can have too much religion?

It has been my privilege as a pastor to counsel with many people who needed deliverance from mental depression. I have found that many of these people needed release from guilt complexes. Their attempts to get release from accusing consciences and the sense of guilt over wrongdoings or a lack of right doing made them "too religious." Paul found such a group in Athens (Acts 17:22). There is a great deal of difference in men's religions and Bible Christianity. Most present-day religion is an attempt to appease God by attending to religious duties. Many people who attend church feel guilty over failures to reach their religious goals. Some ministers bring these people under more condemnation by constantly reminding them of their duties. I recognize a need of

Christians and Their Problems

making men aware of a need for forgiveness. However, Bible Christianity is not a religion of dos and don'ts. It is Christ doing something for and through a man. Jesus said: "For God sent not His Son into the world to condemn the world; but that the world through him might be saved" (John 3:17). "The thief (Satan) cometh not but for to steal, and to kill, and to destroy; I am come that they might have life, and that they might have it more abundantly" (John 10:10). "Come unto me all ye that labor and are heavy laden, and I will give you rest. Take my yoke upon you and learn of me: for I am meek and lowly in heart and you shall find rest unto your souls. For my yoke is easy and my burden is light" (Matthew 11:28–30).

Satan is the destroyer. He is the accuser of the brethren (Revelation 12:10–11). He delights in digging up old sins and dangling them in the faces of God's people. Therefore, many who have been forgiven Satan keeps them under a sense of condemnation. Nothing they do, including church attendance, Bible reading, and other religious duties, gives them peace. **They are too religious.** Some give up to mental depression. All they need to do is accept God's forgiveness and love and be taught to resist these accusing thoughts from the Devil (James 4:7; 2 Corinthians 10:4, 5).

A person can have too much religion but never too much of the life-giving, rest-giving Christ. My advice to your friend is to submit to God's greatest psychiatrist, Jesus Christ (Matthew 11:28, 29) and attend a Bible-believing, faith-building, rest-giving church.

CHAPTER THREE
CHURCH PRACTICES AND BELIEFS

What is meant by the statement, "I plead the Blood of Jesus Christ?" It seems to be a favorite saying in certain prayer groups.

In every fresh spiritual awakening, the theme has been the Blood of Jesus Christ. This present-day outpouring of the Holy Spirit has also brought a new emphasis on the Power and Preciousness of the Blood of Christ (I Peter 1:18–19).

Our enemy, the Devil, is going about like a roaring lion in our day to devour the saints (I Peter 5:8–9). He constantly accuses them and looks for sin in their lives so that he may legally destroy them or their testimony. He opposes their receiving any of God's provisions and blessings. Often times Satan will bring depression and oppression upon a person or a group of people. The greatest weapon against the Devil at such times is the Blood of Jesus Christ. Songs about the Blood like "There Is Power in the Blood," or "What Can Wash Away My Sins?" will defeat the enemy. (Notice the verse that says, "For my cleansing this is my plea, nothing but the Blood of Jesus.") Since we cannot plead our own righteousness, we must plead the Blood of Jesus Christ who is on the Mercy Seat in Heaven. Revelation 12:11 states: "And they overcame him (the Devil) by the Blood of the Lamb."

Since Satan opposes the salvation of souls, a person can be

saved by pleading the Blood of Jesus. Many overcome Satan's opposition to their receiving the Baptism in the Holy Spirit by pleading the Blood. There is indeed Power in the Blood when we testify to our faith in it. If you are sensing opposition from Satan in any area, reverently and persistently plead the Blood of the Lamb, and the victory will come.

Do you think a person can be saved and not go to church?
A person can be married and not live with his family, but it would not be a normal marriage. It could be that a person desires to be with his family, but circumstances prevent it. If he **could** live with his wife and children and does not desire to, I doubt his love for his family. As in natural family ties, a person desires to be with his family; so if a person loves the Lord, he desires to fellowship with the Lord's children, who are his brethren.

I do not know why you asked this question, but my friend, if you have no desire for fellowship with the people who meet for worship, then you need to examine yourself and test the genuineness of your experience with the Lord (2 Corinthians 13:5; I John 3:14; 4:11, 12, 20, 21; Acts 2:41–47).

The New Testament has no record of an isolated Christian who lived to himself (Romans 14:7; 15:2).

(Phone call.) My husband and I are real concerned about our church. Several of the members (including some of the deacons) are dissatisfied with our pastor. They have called for a vote of dismissal for next week. We love our pastor and feel he is God's man, but we do not want to get involved in a church quarrel; therefore, we have decided to stay home the night of the vote. Is this the right thing to do?
"Behold how good and how pleasant it is for brethren to

dwell together in unity" (Psalms 133:1). On the other hand, isn't it tragic when brethren have discord? Personally, I question a system of church government that gives the members of a church—whether mature or immature, and whether spiritual or carnal—the right to call or dismiss a pastor.

Where is the Scripture for such a system? Is this the kind of system that Paul established (Acts 14:23; 20:28)? Is a pastor a paid administrator of the church?

Since dismissing pastors is becoming so common in our day and causes so much trouble, it seems to me that a great deal of prayer and heart-searching needs to be done concerning this matter.

I realize the danger of a pastor becoming overbearing and dictatorial. I am also aware that some ministers do not take the oversight of the flock and feed them properly (I Peter 5:1–4). However, a church that knows how to pray can bring God on the scene to correct such a situation. If a church does not pray and fast about such a serious matter as calling and dismissing a pastor, they deserve anyone they get.

In your particular situation, I believe I would stand behind my pastor. You do not need to get involved in any quarrel; but if this pastor is God's man as you believe he is, he needs you in this critical hour of his life (II Timothy 4:6; Exodus 17:11–13).

Do you believe that God could have created man through the process of evolution?

Some are making an attempt in our day to make the theory of evolution fit into God's creative acts. The theory is called **theistic evolution.**

However, a person could not know the statements and themes of both the Bible and evolutionists and believe both.

What's Your Question?

Even Mr. Huxley, an avowed evolutionist, said: "Evolution, if consistently accepted, makes it impossible to believe the Bible."

Evolution, if it were God's method of creation, would do away with the fall of man, because it teaches steady evolving. A person could not believe in the virgin birth since Christ would be a product of evolution. There would be no room for the cross of Christ and His atoning Blood. Since the term "evolution" means growth and development of the world without supernatural intervention at any point, then theistic evolution would contradict the Bible record of the supernatural in creation.

The theory of evolution commands wide acceptance in our society. Thank God for many Bible-believing school teachers, but a host of teachers in our school system expect children to believe the theory of evolution as fact. The "cave man theory," the "missing link theory," and many other unproven theories are presented as proven facts. Every school pupil should be taught that science has completely abandoned many evolution theories which were so fanatically advanced for several generations. They should also be taught that the law of reproduction is still unbroken. Even though plants and animals have been highly developed through breeding and cultivation, no new species have been produced. In fact, if left to themselves, plants and animals degenerate and certainly do not improve themselves. Ten times the Bible states that each species can reproduce itself and itself only; no earthworm has ever turned into a lizard, scorpion, or snake. The crossing of an ass and a mare will produce a mule, which cannot reproduce itself.

If evolution ever worked, it should be working today, but there is no record of its being in action in the last 6,000 years.

There is much more that could be said to disprove evolu-

Church Practices and Beliefs

tion, but space is limited. Certainly God is not the author of this godless theory.

Man has progressed tremendously in scientific knowledge but according to II Timothy 3:7, man is ever learning but never coming to the knowledge of the truth. Could it be that many who teach that man is on the animal level do so because they themselves live on the beastly level and are making an attempt to salve over their consciences by making themselves believe that man is only a civilized animal?

Jesus said man was made in the Image of God (Matthew 19:4–6). Therefore, He is responsible to be reconciled to his Maker through faith in the Lord Jesus Christ and His cleansing Blood.

What does the Bible mean by "fasting?" Should Christians of our day fast or was this only for Old Testament saints?

Fasting is abstaining from food for a limited time. Its physical purpose is to purge the system of "rubbish." Its spiritual purpose is to seek the Lord with all the heart for some specific need.

Isaiah condemned hypocritical fasting (Isaiah 58) and so did Jesus (Matthew 6); but both practiced fasting. Jesus fasted 40 days before He began His earthly ministry (Matthew 4) and recommends it to present-day disciples (Mark 2:20).

Fasting humbles the soul (Psalms (35:13); brings revival (Nehemiah 1:4); overcomes the Devil (Matthew 4); cures unbelief (Matthew 17:21); gives wisdom (Daniel); puts missionaries on the field (Acts 13:1–3); and delivers from death (Acts 27). The early Methodists fasted on Wednesdays and Fridays and brought awakening to England and America. Isaiah 58 gives many benefits of true fasting.

What's Your Question?

I have been to your worship services and noticed that many lift their hands during the song services. I know there is Scripture for this, but when I have tried it, I feel strange and my arms become very heavy. If this is of the Lord, why do I have so much trouble with it?

Do not feel alone in your difficulty in raising your hands in worship. Most of us have had the same problem. That is why we do not insist on everyone worshipping in this manner.

If we had been taught the following Scriptures from the time we began worshipping the Lord, we would not have developed "inhibitions" about this method of worship:

1. "I will that men pray every where, lifting up holy hands, without wrath and doubting" (I Timothy 2:8). Most Christian leaders have ignored this New Testament command.
2. "Because thy lovingkindness is better than life, my lips shall praise Thee. **Thus** will I bless thee while I live. I will lift up my hands in Thy Name" (Psalms 63:2–3). Lifting up of the hands is to bless the Lord.
3. "Lift up your hands in the sanctuary, and bless the Lord" (Psalms 134:2).
4. "Let my prayer be set forth before thee as incense; and the lifting up of my hands as the evening sacrifice" (Psalms 141:2). Hebrews 13:15 tells us to offer this sacrifice of praise.
5. "I stretch forth my hands unto thee; my soul thirsteth after thee, as a thirsty land" (Psalms 143:6). One mother said she resisted this method of worship until one day her two-year-old son came with lifted hands for her attention. Then she understood better why we lift our hands to our Father.

If we know that the lifting up of the hands in prayer and

Church Practices and Beliefs

praise is God's desire for us, then let us mortify our flesh, which does not wish to be embarrassed, and let us wholeheartedly and earnestly worship God after His order and not worry about man's traditions and inhibitions in worship—the more so if you have the Baptism in the Holy Spirit (Acts 1:4, 5; Acts 2:4).

Why do you observe the first day of the week as a day of worship and a day of rest? Who gave the authority to do so?

I have read and heard that the Catholic church changed the day from Saturday to Sunday, and that the seventh day is the true Bible Sabbath, also the Lord's Day. What is your answer?

In order that one understand the question of the Sabbath, he must learn the difference in the OLD COVENANT and the NEW COVENANT. According to the Scriptures, the Old Covenant expired and a New Covenant was given (Galatians 4:21–31; 5:1–5; Hebrews 7:11–12, 18, 19).

The question is: Does the New Covenant include the Ten Commandments? All the Ten Commandments are given in the New Covenant except one (**1st,** Matthew 22:37; **2nd,** I Corinthians 6:9; **3rd,** Colossians 3:8; **5th, 7th,** Ephesians 6:2; **6th, 10th,** Romans 13:9). The **4th,** which is the Sabbath law, is left out because it was strictly a sign between God and Israel (Exodus 31:13, 18) and because it was a ceremonial law fulfilled in Christ (Hebrews 4:1–11; Colossians 2:14–17).

Sunday keeping was not begun by Constantine in 321 AD or by the Catholic church in 364 AD. The early Christians had a set day to assemble for worship (Hebrews 10:25; I Corinthians 11:17), and according to Acts 20:6–12 and I Corinthians 16:1, 2, this day was the first day of the week. Ignatius, Bishop of Antioch in the first century, wrote: ". . . let every friend of Christ keep the Lord's Day as a festival, the resurrection day, the queen and chief of all days of the week." Justin Martyr wrote in 110 AD "but Sunday is the day on which we hold our common assembly."

I could list several more quotes of early church fathers, but suffice it to say that we celebrate the first day of the week because on that day Jesus arose from the grave gaining victory over death, hell, and Satan and began a New Creation (I Corinthians 5:17). We have entered our rest (Sabbath) in Him (Hebrews 4:7).

Recently I was severely criticized for giving money outside my local church. Should all my tithe and offerings be given where I attend church?

It has been my policy not to attempt to place our people under bondage about their givings. However, I am strongly in favor of local churches. Since I have been saved, I have always given at least one-tenth of my income to "my" local church.

I would be careful about giving God's money to any person or organization that did not distribute a financial statement of income and disbursements. I certainly would not cast reflection on anyone preaching the Gospel. But anyone who is honestly using God's money for God's honor would not object to giving out a public report of income and disbursements, which should be available to all contributors.

It would not be necessary to be so careful about where to give if it were not for religious racketeers who fleece God's people with promises of health, healing, and prosperity for giving to their cause and then they live from "the fat of the land."

It is true that "Give and it shall be given unto you" (Luke 6:38), and "He that soweth sparingly (financially) shall reap also sparingly" (II Corinthians 9:6–8). I believe that every

Church Practices and Beliefs

Christian will be held responsible for being a good steward in the matter of finances. This responsibility includes where he contributes God's money. If your local church is wisely spending God's money to spread the good news of Christ at home and abroad, then I would support it. If your pastor is a Godly man who preaches God's word and undershepherds the flock of God, he deserves your support (I Timothy 5:18). I would not oppose giving to other worthy men, but it isn't fair for men who share no responsibility for a flock and its care to be getting the main part of its offerings (I Corinthians 9:9–14).

Personally, I would not be a part of giving to churches who use God's money to support the Anti-Christ, socialistic move. But I would find a church which makes an honest attempt to honestly use and honestly report the use of contributions.

Do not get under condemnation from the criticisms, but be prayerful and scriptural concerning your tithes and offerings.

Should a woman keep silence in the churches? Explain I Corinthians 14:34–35.

I Corinthians 11:5, 13 records that women can prophesy in public; Acts 2:16–21 records that women spoke in tongues in public; therefore, we must conclude that I Corinthians 14:34 meant silence in some realm other than prophesying or speaking in tongues.

Paul said in I Timothy 2:11–12, "Let the woman learn in silence with all subjection, but I suffer not a woman to teach nor usurp authority over the man but to be in silence."

In plain words, the women are not to set themselves up as authorities in the churches to question the authority of the church leaders who set about to stop confusion and set the church in order. Paul ended Chapter 14 by stating, "Wherefore, brethren, covet to prophesy, and forbid not to speak with tongues. Let all things be done decently and in order."

CHAPTER FOUR

DEMONS

Do you believe in the existence of demons?
The word "demon" is not found in the King James Version of the Bible, but wherever the word "devils" is found it should be translated "demons." There is one "devil" but many "demons." An example in Matthew 8:16: ". . . they brought unto him (Jesus) many that were possessed with devils (demons) and he cast out the spirits with His Word, and healed all that were sick."

Many have denied the existence of demons or evil spirits, but to do so is to deny the Scriptures. Jesus cast over 2,000 demons out of one man (Mark 5:1–15). Mary Magdalene was delivered of seven devils (Luke 8:2).

The early church also cast out devils according to the words of Jesus (Mark 16:17–18). Philip cast out devils and they came out crying with loud voices (Acts 8). Paul cast devils out of a woman in Philippi (Acts 16).

I do not believe that we are to go on a demon search, or to become "demon conscious." Demons will manifest themselves in the presence of the Holy Spirit (Mark 1:23–26). We are to be aware that demons exist and learn how to combat them (Ephesians 6:10–18).

As in Bible days, many today are possessed with unclean spirits, infirm spirits, and countless others. These tormenting spirits are causing mental and physical sickness. The Holy

What's Your Question?

Spirit has been given to the Church to bring deliverance to these oppressed people (Mark 16:17–18; Acts 10:38).

I have many questions in my mind concerning demons. Can a Christian be possessed or deceived by demons? How can you tell if a person has demons? If he has them, how do you deal with them?

Since most Christians are fearful of "ghosts" which cannot be seen, they have chosen to ignore the Scriptures which speak of evil spirits or they simply attribute the Scriptural statements about demons to the superstitions of ignorant people. There are others who attribute every personal problem to evil spirits. Some of these people become demon-conscious and are quick to label people as "demon-possessed."

I feel that both of these positions are harmful to the cause of Christ.

The Scripture declares that we are not to be ignorant of Satan's devices (II Corinthians 2:11). We are to be on guard against evil spirits and be alert to their deceiving methods (Ephesians 6:10–12; I Peter 5:8–9). However, we must be aware that some problems of the inner man are caused by what the Scripture calls "flesh" or "old man" (Galatians 5:17–21). Before we begin discerning evil spirits in others, we must be willing to allow others to apply the same set of standards on us that we use on them. If you are not willing for others to diagnose all of your ugly dispositions as evil spirits, then be very sure you treat others as you would want to be treated. Jesus did not commission us to go "witch hunting." He did give us power to cast out devils when we discern them (Mark 16:17).

To answer your question about demons possessing or deceiving Christians, I shall distinguish between "possessing" and "deceiving." If the definition of possession is "to be con-

Demons

trolled by" then I would say that no Christian can be completely controlled by evil spirits. However, certain areas of a Christian's life may be strongly influenced and controlled by demon forces. Just because a person is indwelt by the Holy Spirit does not mean the Spirit completely controls him. There would be no need for the strong admonitions of the New Testament to be on the alert if it is not possible for evil spirits to invade the life of a believer. When Dr. V. Raymond Edmor of Wheaton College was asked the question you asked, he answered, "Theory says no, but the facts say yes. It is theoretical that a demon cannot possess a body in which the Holy Spirit dwells. However, I know true Christians who were delivered from demons in answer to prayer given in the Name of the Lord Jesus."

It is explicitly stated in the Scriptures that all people are deceived by the Devil until they are born again (Ephesians 2:1-3; Titus 3:5; II Corinthians 4:4). When the person rejects Satan's ways and claims Jesus Christ as his Lord, the glorious light of the gospel shines into his heart and he becomes a child of God. God's Nature is planted in his spirit. He begins a new life (II Peter 1:3; II Corinthians 5:17). What causes much confusion in believers is the fact that his mind and body are not instantly redeemed. There must be a constant renewal of the mind (Ephesians 4:23; Romans 12:1-3). A believer also needs to be filled with the Holy Spirit so that he can be led into ALL truth and equipped with power to overcome the wicked spirits.

The answer to the question about Christians being deceived is—yes, they can and often are. Those who do not judge their own thoughts by the Word of God are subject to be deceived. Our minds are like large living rooms into which evil spirits come without invitation. All truth, learned or revealed, comes from God. Every lie, learned or revealed,

What's Your Question?

comes from Satan. Jesus said, "Ye shall know the truth and the truth shall set you free" (John 8:32). On the other hand, if what you know is a lie, then to that degree you are not free. You can see the importance of knowing God's Word. The first piece of armour mentioned in fighting evil spirits is "truth" (Ephesians 6:14). If our hearts are full of God's Word (Truth) then we can readily discern thoughts given by evil spirits. These thoughts which enslave, defile, and torment are from demons. If they invade the living room of your mind, cast them out by rebuking them in Jesus' Name and by pleading the Blood of Jesus. In order to stay free, renounce all evil and make a total commitment of your body, soul, and spirit unto the Lord Jesus Christ (I Corinthians 12:10).

Do you believe demons exercise greater activity in some areas more than in other areas?

Definitely, yes. In pagan countries where few know the Lord Jesus Christ, there is very little opposition to demon powers. Missionaries who have ministered in pagan countries can vouch for strange manifestations of demon powers and the terrible oppressive spirit of some areas. Many people in the world ignorantly worship Satan and his demon forces (I Corinthians 10:20–21). For example, in oriental countries some people think they are worshipping spirits of their ancestors, when actually they are worshipping evil spirits.

For many years there was little demon activity in this nation as compared with heathen nations. The Bible was read in almost every classroom. This nation, though never entirely Christian, had a respect for God, the Bible, and morality. However, with the removal of the Bible and prayer from our schools and homes, the Devil has gained much strength in our land. Many people are being oppressed and possessed by demon forces all over the USA. I believe there is a definite

Demons

connection between demons and the spreading of such drugs as LSD, speed, amphetamines, etc. There is also a connection in the crime wave, violence, homosexuality, long hair on males and demon activity. Since we have always associated demon activity with paganism, we must define paganism. The best way I know to define it is by its fruits, which are: lawlessness, nudity, rock and roll music in a minor key, sexual perversion, and ignorance of the Bible. These things are prevalent in all barbarian lands. America is fast becoming pagan and is in need of deliverance. It is the responsibility of God's people to rise up and declare the power of Jesus' Name and His Blood to set men free from these demonic forces (Revelation 12:11). The main reason for the present-day move of the Holy Spirit is to restore the body of Christ to the supernatural power of its early days so as to raise up a standard against the flood of the enemy (Isaiah 59:19). The answer is not Washington marches; nor is it psychiatry, education, or just the letter of God's Word. The answer is the full gospel delivered under the anointing of the Holy Spirit. Amen and amen!

How does a person cast out demons that are in another person?

1. Do not attempt to enter this ministry without training in the wiles of the Devil and unless you can discern evil spirits. All believers have authority over demons, but all do not have discernment nor are they spiritually ready for this ministry (Matthew 17:20–21). 2. Be sure that the person desires deliverance. If he doesn't, then pray for a change of his mind. 3. Make the person who desires deliverance understand Satan's defeat at Calvary and convince him of the Victory that is in Jesus Christ. (I have noticed that some keep reminding Satan of his defeat. That is unnecessary since he already knows and

What's Your Question?

trembles when others realize it (James 2:19). Satan knows when you are convinced, and also when you are bluffing.) There is no magic formula for casting out evil spirits. The sons of Sceva tried this method and miserably failed (Acts 19). Your faith in what Jesus has done brings victory when you speak the word of faith. 4. Be filled with the Holy Spirit. Jesus cast out demons by the Spirit of God (Matthew 12:28). 5. Boldly quote the Words of God against Satan as Jesus did (Matthew 4). Remember, however, that the Word of God is the sword of the Spirit and not our own sword. The anointing breaks the yoke (Isaiah 10:27; Luke 4:18). 6. Say: "In the Name of Jesus Christ, I command you evil spirits to depart." Stand your ground without wavering. Evil spirits know that they must submit to a Spirit-filled person who knows he has authority in the Name of Jesus (Mark 6:7). Expect them to leave. THEY WILL! Victory is certain through our resurrected Lord.

CHAPTER FIVE

DENOMINATIONAL QUESTIONS

The question I am about to ask is not based on something I heard or read, it is based on existing and undisputable facts. I think this is a logical and reasonable question, and it certainly comes from an honest and sincere heart. Falsehood has an infinity of combinations; but the truth has only one mode of being. If the Bible is the inspired Word of God, and not a product of the physical mind, then tell me how learned men have been able to organize some hundred or so combinations of religions out of one and the same Book? I need a teacher, one who can give me a logical explanation. I want facts that will stand the light of intelligent investigation. I am tired of fantasy. I am weary of being burdened down with theories. I want facts. Thank you for your answer.

I appreciate your letter and will attempt to give a simple answer which I pray will help clear up your **confusion.** I do not know all the answers to your question of the many "religions" which have been organized from the Bible. I do know that I, too, sought for truth (reality) and found a person—Jesus Christ, the Lord (John 14:6). Since that time—February, 1947—the Scriptures have had real meaning to me. Thousands could give this same testimony.

I'm sure that our Lord has been grieved by the divisions among those who claim to believe the same book. Dr. Torrey said, "In the present imperfect state of man, where no indi-

What's Your Question?

vidual is large enough to take in the whole scope of God's truth, and where one man sees one line of truth strongly and another man another line of truth, denominations have been necessary. But it is well that denominational lines are now fast sinking out of sight and each denomination is coming to understand and accept truths for which other denominations have stood."

False cults have also arisen from certain Scriptures misused and taken out of context. Even Satan tried this method with Christ (Luke 4:10). The common denominator for all denominations is faith in Christ Jesus (I John 4:1–3). He was born of a virgin, proved He was from God by many miracles and words (John 20:30–31), died for our sins (I Peter 2:24), arose from the grave on the third day (John 20 and 21; I Corinthians 15), now lives as our mediator (I John 2:1; Hebrews 7:25), and shall return to receive us to Himself (John 14:1–6; I Thessalonians 4:13–17; Revelation 1:7).

If you will submit yourself to Christ Jesus and ask Him to give a witness in your heart that He is alive, He will do so. "For whosoever shall call upon the Name of the Lord shall be delivered" (Romans 10:13). "If any man will do His will he shall know of the doctrine (teaching) . . ." (John 7:17).

Begin now to read the Gospel of John slowly and deliberately and ask God to reveal Christ to you.

Are Baptists Protestants? I have a friend who says that Baptists were not a part of the Protestant movement in the Middle Ages. He says they were never a part of the Catholic Church but originated in the first century. Have you read the book The Trail of Blood? **Is it true?**

Those who have studied church history objectively know that there was no Christian Church by the name of "Baptist" until after the Protestant Reformation in the 16th Century. A group called "Anabaptists" apparently originated in Switzerland from the Zwingli Movement in 1519. The name was used in derision because they "re-baptized." They later were named "Baptists" or "Baptizers."

Several Christian groups, including some Baptists, have laid claim to being in existence in unbroken succession since the Church was established by Christ. It is true that there have always been groups of Christians who were persecuted by organized religion and were considered "outside the gate" (Hebrews 13:11-13). However, none of these groups were called by names of any present-day denominations. Some would teach that though these groups were not called "Baptist" they were Baptists in everything but name. Other groups claim the same for their denominations. Those who make these claims often appeal to prejudice and pride.

The Trail of Blood could be a good book if it were not written from a sectarian viewpoint. Christ has always had followers, who though not always unified in doctrinal detail, loved Him enough to be ostracized and martyred for His Name's sake. What does it matter what name was given to them? Jesus said, "Where two or three are gathered IN (not by) my Name, there am I in the midst of them" (Matthew 18:20).

It seems to me that it is a sign of spiritual deterioration when any church is more interested in where they came from than their present state of spirituality and their destination.

How did you come to believe as you do? Were you always a Baptist? Please tell some of your religious educational background.

I was raised in a Southern Baptist home; baptized at age twelve by a Southern Baptist preacher; and converted at age twenty in Richards Memorial Methodist Church, Pensacola, Florida, under Reverend Ed Hardin.

What's Your Question?

I attended Brother Ed's Alma Mater, Bob Jones University, from 1951–1955. During that time, I returned to the Southern Baptist Convention and was ordained a Southern Baptist minister in 1954. I pastored Hill Top Baptist Church, and Airport Baptist Church, Greenville, South Carolina; New Hope Baptist Church, Sumrall, Mississippi; the First Baptist Church, Clara, Mississippi; and Boulevard Baptist Church, Pensacola, Florida—all Southern Baptist Churches. During those years I received the B.A. from William Carey College, Hattiesburg, Mississippi; the M.S. from the University of Southern Mississippi; and the M.R.E. from New Orleans Baptist Theological Seminary. I received the Baptism in the Holy Spirit while pastoring Boulevard Baptist Church, February 9, 1964. Liberty Baptist Church was founded in March, 1964, and Liberty Bible College in February, 1966.

Does it really matter what we believe so long as we are all trying to reach the same place? I know good people of all religions. Won't we all go to Heaven so long as we try to be good?

According to the Scriptures, a person must be completely righteous in order to go to heaven (Galatians 3:10–12). But the Bible also says that "none are righteous" (Romans 3:10). God's problem was how to make unrighteous people righteous.

II Corinthians 5:21 tells us how He provided righteousness for all. "For He hath made Him (Jesus) to be sin for us, who knew no sin that we might be made righteousness of God in Him."

Jesus became sin that we may be righteous. So righteousness has been provided. However, not all have obtained it. Some are still trying to make themselves fit for fellowship with God. Romans 10:3, "For they being ignorant of God's righteousness, and going about to establish their own right-

Denominational Questions

eousness have not submitted themselves unto the righteousness of God." These people will not be able to fellowship with God nor enter heaven because they do not have God's salvation. Jesus said: "I am the Way" (John 14:6). Peter said: "Neither is there salvation in any other; for there is none other name under heaven given among men, whereby we must be saved" (Acts 4:12).

In order to have righteousness, every person must submit himself to God's plan for righteousness and be saved. Romans 10:9 tells how to receive salvation and righteousness. "If thou shalt confess with thy mouth the Lord Jesus, and shalt believe in thine heart that God raised Him from the dead, thou shalt be saved. For with the heart man believeth unto righteousness; and with the mouth confession is made unto salvation."

Yes, it does matter what we believe! The difference is righteousness and life versus sin and hell. If you desire righteousness, believe that Jesus shed His blood for you and is risen again.

Confess Him now and make Him your Lord and He will become your Saviour. God's peace will come into your heart as He imparts His life to you.

For further instruction on God's way of righteousness, read chapters 1–10 of Romans and Galatians 3.

CHAPTER SIX

EMOTIONALISM AND GOD

This question is not intended to cast any reflection on those of our day who are entering into what is called the Charismatic Revival. In fact, I am very hungry to see the real move of God for our day. But why is there so much in the present-day movement that seems fleshly and unreal? If this move is of God, why all the defects and weaknesses among those participating? How can a person feel free to enter into a movement when he sees things within it that obviously are not of God?

No doubt, your question is one which many honest, sincere Christians have on their hearts. In fact, this was my "hang-up" for a while.

It would be great if God could give us a perfect manifestation of Himself in any spiritual awakening. The problem is: "We have this treasure in earthen vessels" (II Corinthians 4:7). God must reveal Himself through imperfect human vessels.

The present-day revival is going through about the same experiences that all revivals have. For example, Acts reveals imperfections in the early church awakening. The revivals under Luther, Wesley, Finney and others had their difficulties with fleshly and satanic demonstrations. John Wesley wrote of the revival from which the Methodist church originated: "Almost as soon as I was gone, two or three began to take their imaginations for impressions from God. Meantime, a flood of reproach came upon me almost from every quarter . . ." He once prayed: "Oh, Lord, send us old time revival without the defects; but if this cannot be, send it with all its defects. We must have revival." We must also remember that during times of spiritual declension, church worship and activity are usually far from the Bible pattern. Therefore, when revival brings the church back to Bible pattern, it is difficult for those accustomed to religious traditions to adjust to the Bible pattern of worship and ministry. Religious flesh cringes at anything that seems unsophisticated.

Many missed the visitation of God when Jesus was on the earth because they judged the visitation by those who followed Jesus, and because it did not fit into their conception of God's promised revelation of Himself (Luke 19:41-44).

I wish I could tell you that everything that is happening today in the Name of the Holy Spirit is genuine. It isn't! May God give us wisdom to separate between the precious and the vile (Jeremiah 15:19) and "to prove all things and hold fast to that which is good" (I Thessalonians 5:21).

I am in a search for a deeper walk with God and for more meaningful worship, but I fear in my search that I will give over to emotionalism. Aren't we commanded by the Scriptures to be in control of our emotions? Isn't there a danger in letting ourselves go?

I believe that emotions have a very vital and legitimate place in worship. Anyone who reads the Bible with an open heart must see the part that emotions had in the lives of the saints.

For example, read the account of Mary's worship of Jesus at the house of Simon the leper. Compare Simon's cold approach to Mary's sincere emotional manifestation of her love. Jesus said of her, "She hath washed my feet with tears

Emotionalism and God

and wiped them with the hairs of her head . . . this woman since the time I came in hath not ceased to kiss my feet" (Luke 7:44-45).

Emotionalism is only wrong when alone. Jesus describes in Mark 4 the emotional, superficial hearers who bring no fruit to perfection. When promises are made in the heat of emotions that are not carried through, emotionalism becomes superficial. Matthew 21:28-31 gives such an account of a young man who was stirred in his heart and said "I will go" and went not. Emotions certainly have no Christian value unless connected with right conduct. However, the worship experience that does not touch the emotions does not touch the whole person.

David, a man after God's own heart, worshipped emotionally. Read the Psalms of the hand raising (Psalms 134), hand-clapping (Psalms 47), and music-inspired worship (Psalms 150). David danced before the Lord with all his might. Michal, his wife, despised his show of his emotions (II Samuel 6:14-16, 20-33). God showed His displeasure not to David but to Michal, and He dried up her womb. I have seen God dry up the wombs of churches, and they bring forth no newborn babes because of their scorn of emotionalism and their exchange of real worship for music appreciation and literary evaluation.

God's people in our society are emotionally starved because of the lack of release in spiritual worship. It is time, my friend, to shake yourself free from inhibitions caused by excessive concern about what others think. Forget social "taboos" and worship the Lord with your whole being. Mary, at Simon's house, was so deeply moved by the Love of the Lord that she ceased not to kiss His feet. She cared not for the critics. Her primary concern, as should be ours, was to express her deep love for her Master.

What's Your Question?

Recently I visited your church services. While I enjoyed the good spirit among you, I was surprised to hear stringed instruments, hand-clapping during the singing, and see several people raising their hands while worshipping. I am not against these things, but they seem a bit out of place in a church worship service. Could this be emotionalism? Please explain your concept of reverence in worship.

I am glad that you enjoyed the spirit of our services, and I am not surprised at your reaction to our type praise and worship. My reaction was the same as yours when I first entered a church where real joy was expressed. I thought it was out of place. However, I could not find Scriptures to support my position. On the contrary, I found many Scriptures which changed my concept of worship.

"So David and all the house of Israel brought up the Ark of the Lord with shouting and with the sound of the trumpet. Michal saw King David leaping and dancing before the Lord; and she despised him in her heart" (II Samuel 6:16). Evidently God thought David was a man after His own heart (Acts 13:22). God dried up Michal's womb to show His disapproval of her attitude.

"O clap your hands all ye people; shout unto God with the voice of triumph" (Psalms 147). "Pray every where, lifting up holy hands" (I Timothy 2:8). Luke 19:37–40 reveals the attitude of Jesus toward rejoicing and praising the Lord. Revelation 7:9–11 reveals future worship in Heaven. Psalms 150 lists the type instruments with which to praise the Lord.

The Scriptures are plain that God loves the praise of His people. He has promised to manifest His presence during our praises (Psalms 22:3). He especially loves praise of the heart coming forth through our lips. Worship can be in quietness and many times there is a quietness and peace during our

Emotionalism and God

worship services. At other times joy is manifested through exuberant praise.

I have observed that many who are really expressive at ball games are deathly quiet during church services. Sometimes this is caused by the teaching that church is no place to express our emotions. Other times it is because people love games better than they love the Lord. Could it be that many **worship** at ball games and **endure** the church services? Our worship, whether it be for the Lord or ball or other things will be expressed by our entire being, including our emotions.

As you no doubt noticed, not all raise their hands, clap their hands, etc., during our worship services. As others feel free to express themselves this way, please feel free not to do so when you visit with us. We are taught not to judge others but to love those who express themselves differently than we do.

The Scriptures repeatedly tell us to rejoice in the Lord. A rejoicing person seldom gets sick because "a merry heart doeth good like medicine" (Proverbs 17:22). "Let us offer the sacrifice of praise to God continually, that is, the fruit of our lips, giving thanks to His Name" (Hebrews 13:15).

CHAPTER SEVEN
ETERNITY ISSUES

Do you believe in the doctrine of eternal security—that is, "once saved, always saved?"

It would be impossible for me to give in this brief article the pros and cons of keeping or losing one's salvation. To simply state my position without Scriptural reasons would only tend to promote prejudice and would not be wise; therefore, you may find my answer in a book entitled **Life in the Son,** written by Reverend Robert Shank, Southern Baptist pastor of Louisburg Baptist Church, Louisburg, Missouri, and distributed by the Westcott Publishers, Springfield, Missouri. The introduction in the book is written by Dr. William W. Adams, professor in the Southern Baptist Theological Seminary, Louisville, Kentucky. Note the following quotes from the analysis of the book: **"Life in the Son** appears in a time of confusion in ecclesiastical polity. There are nearly three hundred separate denominations in America today . . . (which) must in part be attributed to doctrinal confusion. . . . The appearance of such a book will be welcomed by all men who care more for unity of the Spirit and of the faith and the knowledge of the Son of God than for the defense of creed and dogma. . . . There are certain people who should not read **Life in the Son**: people who have already decided what they intend to believe and who only read for confirmation of their present opinion should not read Mr. Shank's

What's Your Question?

book. The book was not written for people with spring-trap minds that have already sprung.

"On the other hand, there are certain people who should read it: people whose first loyalty is to the Scriptures rather than traditional interpretations . . . people who are ready to accept and follow the truth, whatever it is and wherever it leads. . . . I wish it were in my power to place a copy of **Life in the Son** into the hands of every pastor, teacher, leader, and layman who sincerely loves the Bible, the Saviour, the Church, and the fulness of Spiritual life."

You may order this book from Liberty Bible College Bookstore, P. O. Box 3138, Pensacola, Florida (price $4.95 plus postage and handling, total $5.50; 380 pages).

Do you believe that the heathen who never hear the Gospel will be lost?

The Scriptures say that they are already lost. Jesus did not come to condemn the world but to save them from condemnation (John 3:17; Luke 19:10). If a sick person dies, he dies because he is sick, not because he didn't hear of a medicine. The medicine could have saved him, but he died of the sickness. Likewise, a sinner is lost because he is a sinner, not because he has not heard of a remedy (Romans 2:14–15).

Let us reason by logic. If the heathen will be saved who never hear the gospel, we would do them an injustice to preach the gospel to them. Why? Because if they hear and reject the gospel they could not be saved. So they would have 100% chance of going to Heaven if the heathen who never hear will be saved. Surely no sensible person believes we should stop preaching the gospel to the heathen.

Jesus died on the cross to save sinners, which include the heathen (I Timothy 1:15). There is no such thing as a limited atonement which would mean that Christ died for a limited

Eternity Issues

number of people. There is no sinner for whom Christ did not die (II Corinthians 5:14, 15; Titus 2:11; I Timothy 2:6). Jesus died even for those who deny Him (II Peter 2:1). Jesus desires all to be saved (II Peter 3:9).

But every person must personally believe in Jesus Christ before he can be saved (Acts 4:12; Romans 10:9-15). "But how shall they hear without a preacher?" (verse 14).

Jesus gave us the commission to go and preach the gospel to every creature (Matthew 28:19-20). The heathen are our responsibility. We have the remedy because we have the name through which they can be saved. Without that name, they cannot be saved (Acts 4:12). Those who hear and believe will be saved.

This makes the commission of Jesus in Matthew 28:19, 20 and Acts 1:4, 5, 8 ever so important.

Do you believe that God sends people to an eternal lake of fire? It is hard for me to believe that I could do such a thing. Isn't God more merciful than we are?

Yes! God is more merciful than we are. Nothing is more graphically pictured in the Scriptures than the Love of God. **God so Loved!**

Would you give your son for a sinning world? God did! God so loves and is so merciful that He forgives and saves sinners that receive Jesus Christ as Lord (John 3:16).

"Hell" is not a pleasant subject, but the ever-loving Son of God mentioned it often. (Matthew 5:22, 29-30; 10:28; 18:9; 23:23; 25:41; Mark 9:3-37; Luke 16:23 and many other Scriptures tell of Jesus' knowledge of Hell.) He wept over those who made no effort to escape the torments of Hell.

I don't understand all about the eternal punishment of the impenitent, but I'm sure that God's Word is truthful. Unwelcome facts remain facts. It is possible to reason Hell out of

What's Your Question?

one's mind, but not out of existence. Shallow views of sin and the holiness of God cause men to doubt the justice of eternal punishment. Let us realize that man is the only creature created in the image of God. His sin against God was treason! He sided with the Devil against God. Hell was made for the Devil and his angels. Unless man repents and changes his lord from Satan to Jesus, and is regenerated by the Spirit of God, then he, too, will hear the terrible words, "Depart from me, ye cursed, into everlasting fire, prepared for the Devil and his angels" (Matthew 25:41).

The same Bible that says, "God is love" (I John 4:16) also says, "God is light" (I John 1:5); "He (God) is righteous" (I John 2:29); and "Our God is a consuming fire" (Hebrews 12:29). "Behold the goodness and severity of God" (Romans 11:22).

It is because I believe the Scriptures that I answered God's call and I have given my life to preaching the gospel of Jesus Christ by radio, printed page, in churches, on the streets, here and in foreign lands to as many as will hear in order that they be saved and conformed to the Image of Christ. (Read 2 Peter 2 and 3 for a better understanding of God's love and wrath.)

What does the Bible mean in Romans 8:29, "For whom he did foreknow, he also did predestinate to be conformed to the image of his son"? Another similar verse is found in Ephesians 1:4 and 5. Do you believe that God chooses only certain ones to be saved?

Whatever else predestination means, it cannot mean that God will only save certain people that He has chosen beforehand and will not save anyone else.

I believe that God has predestined every child of God to become like Jesus, but it is up to each individual whether or not he becomes a child of God (John 3:15–20; Revelation 22:17; I Timothy 2:4; II Peter 3:9).

God preplanned that Adam and Eve would become like Jesus, but Satan interfered. But "God so loved the world that He gave His only begotten Son that whosoever believeth in Him should have everlasting life." It was this plan that He foreknew and foreordained and not man's conformity to the plan. He foreordained that each one who accepts His plan, which is receiving Jesus Christ as Lord, receives eternal life. He has also pre-arranged that all who reject Him will be cast into Hell.

Notice in Ephesians 1:4 we are chosen in Christ. Those who abide in Christ are predestined to become like Him. But it is up to each person to repent and believe into Christ.

God has a plan for your life and mine, but we must make the choice whether we will do His will. He then will place His life in us and give us power to do His will.

CHAPTER EIGHT
COMMENTS, EXPLANATIONS

Is it in the Bible where a little nation will rise up in the East and rule the world until the end of time?

I know of no Scripture which states that a little nation of the East shall rule the world at the end of time. There are many passages which deal with the anti-Christ system and the person of the anti-Christ who will rise to power in the last days.

There are different and some strange ideas about the anti-Christ. I believe the world is fast getting ready emotionally, morally, economically, and politically for a strong personality who is described in 2 Thessalonians 2 and Revelation 13 and other chapters. He will become an international idol who will have the answers to man's greedy desires. He will promote fortune-telling, palm reading, crystal gazing, astrology, and E.S.P. (Revelation 13). The masses will turn (multitudes already have) to the evils of spiritualism.

God's people who are alert will not be drawn into the schemes of this anti-Christ system. We are the children of the light (I Thessalonians 5). Let us watch and pray, for the coming of our Lord draweth nigh (Matthew 24:33, 42; James 5:8–9).

Explain I Corinthians 7:1–2, 9, 36–38. Does God prefer that man and woman not marry at all?

What's Your Question?

Please notice verse 26—"present distress." Chapter 7 of I Corinthians concerns marriage and sex. It is especially written to Christian workers during times of persecution. Marriage is not condemned, but marriage of Christian ministers during times of distress is likely to add to their difficulties. However, even in times of distress, God demands purity and chastity among His people. Hebrews 13:4 says, "Marriage is honorable in all, and the bed (sexual intercourse of man and wife) undefiled: but whoremongers and adulterers God will judge." If a person, even a Christian minister, cannot control his sexual desires, he had best get married (I Corinthians 7:7, 9). It seems to me that verses 7, 9, 20, 28, 32, 33 and 35 are speaking primarily to Christian ministers and missionaries. A Christian minister, especially during times of persecution, should have as few distractions as possible; however, nowhere do the Scriptures forbid marriage of a minister (I Timothy 4:1-3). Since sexual incompatibility and infidelity are the main reasons for divorce in our time, I feel it would be helpful to every Christian couple to read I Corinthians 7 in order that they may understand their sexual responsibilities one to another. For the Scriptures pertaining to marriage, read Matthew 19:1-2; Ephesians 5:22-23; and I Peter 3:1-9.

In the past few centuries man's brutal and piercing assault upon the material or physical world has produced astounding results in which many old cherished beliefs were abandoned and multitudes of nature's secrets unlocked for the betterment of mankind.

Now if the same energetic effort and uncompromising mental scrutiny were applied to the spiritual world, do you think we could expect similar results?

I have had some difficulty deciding exactly what you mean by your question. If you mean that by human effort and

Comments, Explanations

human reasoning we can find spiritual answers, then I would answer "no" (I Corinthians 1:17–29). If you are asking should we change our old-fashioned beliefs in the Scriptures for some modern methods to attempt to meet human spiritual needs, my answer would still be "no."

However, if you are asking should we seek God in prayer and in His Word for the revealing of spiritual laws which will help meet needs, then my answer is definitely "yes" (I Corinthians 2:12)! For example, Paul said, "For the LAW of the Spirit of life in Christ Jesus hath made me free from the law of sin and death" (Romans 8:2).

As there are certain laws that men have discovered in the natural realm that have, as you said, "produced astounding results," so there are spiritual laws given to us in the Scriptures that produce even greater results in the spiritual realm. For example, some are learning that the law of faith operates today as it did when the Gospels were written or when Peter and Paul were on earth (Romans 3:27). Jesus said, "All things are possible to them which believe" (Mark 9:23). Those words are for any time. There is no need for something new in religious circles. Millions are returning to the simple primitive faith that our Lord taught, and it is working! Because of this, these same people are abandoning **old, cherished** dispensational traditions that teach that God does not work miracles now as He once did. Every month 750 Full Gospel Businessmen's meetings and hundreds of Full Gospel churches are witnessing miraculous new births in people that bring joy and peace unspeakable. They also witness God healing all kinds of sicknesses and diseases. Others are being filled with the Holy Spirit. This is the Lord's doings and it is marvelous in our eyes (Mark 12:11). Are these the results of which you speak?

What's Your Question?

Can you explain why so many preachers go wrong? If a minister can't walk straight, who can be expected to?

In proportion to the number of ministers, relatively few fall by the wayside. However, it is always serious when any professing Christian does wrong, but more especially when a minister becomes immoral or a cheat. But a minister falls for the same reasons others have fallen: Saul—pride and stubbornness; David—lack of watchfulness (II Samuel 11); Peter—lack of prayer and self-confidence (Matthew 26:40-41; Luke 22:33-34); and Judas—love of money (John 12:5-6).

We are told to take heed lest we fall (I Corinthians 10:12). As ministers we are told to give no offense in anything lest the ministry be blamed (II Corinthians 6). Praise God for every minister who is heeding this advice. May God bless them. Those who are dishonest with debts, immoral, etc., will give a strict account unto God (Matthew 7:22-23; Romans 14:12-13; II Corinthians 5:10-11).

However, since man is fallible and subject to fall, we must keep our eyes upon Jesus our Lord (Hebrews 2:2). He is able to keep us from falling (Jude 24).

If Mark 16:17 is for today, then why don't modern day proclaimers of this verse prove that they believe it by handling poisonous snakes, and then we will believe them.

A close examination of your statements will reveal that it is very near what Satan said to Jesus about jumping off the temple (Luke 4:9-12). He even quoted Scripture to prove his point; however, Jesus never jumped off the temple nor worked any other miracle to prove His power to unbelievers. Paul had an experience with a poisonous snake (Acts 28:3-6), but there is no record of early Christians deliberately handling snakes as proof of their faith. Their ministry was to pro-

Comments, Explanations

claim the Good News and to build faith in the Word of God.

Personally, I feel that theirs was a much more profitable ministry than the one of destroying faith in the Word by ridiculous statements. Jesus said that these signs would follow believers. "All things are possible to them that believe" (Mark 9:23). The Lord continues to confirm His Word to and through believers (Mark 16:20).

What do you think of the rock opera, "Jesus Christ, Superstar"? One of our Pensacola schools is using this record for intensive and lengthy study.

"Jesus Christ, Superstar" is one of the most blasphemous works of our time.

God the Father is actually made a tool of the Devil in the opera, to kill His Son, Jesus. In turn, God the Father uses Judas Iscariot as His tool for his own sadistic desires. Jesus is presented as a weak, self-pitying humanitarian who does not know why he is treated so cruelly by His Father and by society in general.

The unbelieving authors of the opera make Christ say to the Father, "Can you show me now that I would not be killed in vain? Show me just a little of Your Omnipresent Brain. Show me there is a reason for Your wanting me to die. You were too keen on where and how and not so hot on why . . . God, Thy will is hard, but You hold every card. I will drink Your cup of poison; nail me to the cross and break me, bleed me, beat me, kill me, take me now—before I change my mind."

Contrast that human reasoning with Matthew 16:21, "From that time forth Jesus began to shew unto his disciples, how that he must . . . be killed and be raised the third day." (See also Matthew 17:12; Luke 19:10; John 3:14–15). Jesus knew why He was to die. He could have called twelve legions

What's Your Question?

of angels to prevent His crucifixion (Matthew 26:53). Jesus also said that He voluntarily gave His life for His sheep (John 19:15). He added that no man could take His life from Him. Jesus "bare our sins in His own body on the tree" (I Peter 2:24). Paul added: "For the preaching of the cross is to them that perish foolishness; but unto us which are saved it is the power of God" (I Corinthians 1:18–25). See also Philippians 2:5–8.

Throughout the opera Jesus is presented as suffering because of the "establishment." The apostles are portrayed as greedy idiots. Only sinful Mary Magdalene **sympathizes** with Jesus. The opera indeed presents another Jesus other than the one given by the Father to redeem the world.

May God have mercy on our school system if it allows this kind of anti-Christian brainwashing material to be studied in our classrooms and forbids the study of the Bible.

Could I have committed the unpardonable sin? I cannot get an answer from the Lord for overcoming a certain evil in my life. Would you please explain the unpardonable sin?

According to Mark 3:28–30 and Matthew 12:31–32, the unpardonable sin is blaspheming or speaking against the Holy Spirit.

It is attributing the supernatural works of the Holy Spirit to the work of evil spirits.

I do not believe that you have committed this sin. The 6th, 7th and 8th chapters of Romans deal with your problem. A man under bondage cried out, "What I hate, that I do . . . O wretched man that I am, who shall deliver me . . . ? I thank God through Jesus Christ our Lord." Along with your praying, start believing and confessing these words: "Jesus Christ died, was buried and was raised again for me. I iden-

Comments, Explanations

tify myself with Jesus Christ, confessing Him as my Lord; therefore sin shall not have dominion over me. I now take dominion over sin through Jesus Christ my Lord. Jesus Christ gives me power over sin and I will not yield my body as an instrument of sin. The Law of the Spirit of life in Christ Jesus has made me free from the law of sin and death" (Romans 6:4, 6, 11–14, and 8:2). It is not the prayer of doubt but the prayer and confession of faith that makes us overcomers. "This is the victory that overcomes the world, even our faith" (I John 5:4). Two other wonderful verses to memorize are: "For the weapons of our warfare are not carnal, but mighty through God to the pulling down of strong holds; casting down imaginations . . . and bringing into captivity every thought to the obedience of Christ" (II Corinthians 10:4, 5).

Confess this: "These evil imaginations and thoughts shall not have dominion over me. I now cast them out and will think pure thoughts" (Philippians 4:8). Hold fast to the confession of your faith without wavering (Hebrews 10:23); seek for the fullness of the Holy Spirit (Ephesians 5:18); and get under the teaching of a faith-building church. The victory is yours! Claim it.

I notice the word "selah" is written often in the Psalms. What does it mean?

The word is derived from a Hebrew word which means "to be silent." It signifies a pause in the singing of the psalms while the instrument played an interlude.

Two weeks ago I answered a question in the News Journal on whether God would send people to Hell. The answer brought some favorable response and some not so favorable. One response was: "In your article you misrepresented our Lord Jesus Christ and His teachings. Every person who is honest and educated knows that our Lord in Matthew 5:22 had no reference to Hell. The valley of Hinnon was located outside the city.

"This valley was where the Hebrews took their children and ran them through the fire and burned them alive on the altar of Tophet. Josiah destroyed the heathen altars and made a garbage heap out of the valley. Dead animals and executed criminals were placed there in the fire. Worms were always present . . ." This man said this was the place Jesus was referring to. Another response was: "You ought to be in jail for trying to scare people . . ." No doubt both these letters came from sincere people. What was said about the Valley of Hinnon being a place of burning garbage and worms is true. Jesus used this valley only to describe the final doom of the impenitent (Matthew 5:22, 29; 10:28; 18:9; Mark 9:43). As proof He was not referring literally to this garbage dump, He said in Matthew 25:41, "Depart from me, ye cursed, into everlasting fire prepared for the Devil and his angels." Was the garbage dump prepared for the Devil and his angels? Another proof among many is in Revelation 19:20, which describes the punishment of the anti-Christ and the false prophet. My question is, "Will they be cast on the garbage dump outside Jerusalem?" If so, will they still be alive there 1,000 years later? (Revelation 20:10.)

I have no desire to argue nor to scare people but only to be faithful to my task as a watchman to warn those who have not submitted themselves to God's Son that they are now under condemnation and the wrath of God (John 3:16–19, 36). Fear is not a bad motive since "Noah moved with fear and built an ark" (Hebrews 11:17). "The fear of the Lord is the beginning of knowledge" (Proverbs 1:7).

"There is therefore now no condemnation to them which

are in Christ Jesus" (Romans 8:1). "How shall we escape if we neglect so great salvation?" (Hebrews 2:3.)

Should Christians celebrate Christmas when it has been proven that Christ was not born in December and that it originated as a pagan holiday?

I do not know when Christ was born and I doubt that any man does. The fact that heathen had holidays during this season does not prove that Christmas was a joint celebration with the pagans.

There are many things that I personally do not cherish about the Christmas holidays. (1) More liquor is drunk during this season than at any other time of the year. (2) Many businesses think of Christmas only as a time to make money, and (3) many of God's people give more expensive Christmas presents to others than they do to Jesus, whose birthday is to be celebrated.

However, I love many things about the season. People's hearts are generally more tender during this season. Christ's name is heard in many areas through the Christmas carols, plays, and Christmas sermons. I think we do well to have a day of rejoicing over the virgin birth of our Saviour. If we have **any day** to glorify Christ, it will be a day somebody else has used for bad purposes. Every day belongs to our Lord, including December 25th. If someone else has a wrong motive for celebrating Christmas, let us leave them for God to judge. Let us do good and take advantage of this season to preach "glad tidings of great joy." If someone else does make a god out of Christmas trees and lights, we will use them only as a symbol of joy and gladness in our hearts for our "Emmanuel." Romans 14:5, 6a: "One man esteemeth one day above another: another esteemeth every day alike. Let every

What's Your Question?

man be fully persuaded in his own mind. He that regardeth the day regardeth it unto the Lord, and he that regardeth not the day, to the Lord he doth not regard it."

If you regard Christmas, regard it to the Lord. If you regard it not, do it as to the Lord. But let nobody be critical of others who regard Christmas as a special time of worship of our Lord Jesus.

We wish all of our readers a very merry Christmas. Thanks for the wonderful response to these articles and your expressions of appreciation.

CHAPTER NINE

GLOSSALALIA

I have heard you and others mention a Charismatic (Is that the way you spell it?) Revival in our day. Could you explain the meaning of this term?

Yes, that is the correct spelling. The New Testament word "charis" is translated **gift** or **grace**. When we speak of the Charismatic Revival, we mean a revival of the gifts of the Holy Spirit mentioned in I Corinthians 12:7–10, i.e., (1) the Word of Wisdom, supernatural wisdom given instantaneously for any particular circumstance (Acts 27:20–26). (2) The Word of Knowledge, a companion to the Word of Wisdom. It is seen in II Kings 3 and Acts 5. (3) Faith, a supernatural faith for a particular need (Acts 14:9–10). (4) Miracles, a demonstration of God's power which alters the laws of nature (I Kings 3:4; Acts 9:36–42). (5) Gifts of Healing (notice plural "gifts"), supernatural working of the Holy Spirit in healings of diseases. No human abilities are involved in these kinds of healings (Acts 3:5, 8, etc.). (6) Prophecy, it can be used generally and specifically, but when defined as a gift of the Holy Spirit, it is inspired utterance which is given for edification, exhortation, and comfort (I Corinthians 14:3). (7) Discerning of Spirits, supernatural ability to discern the source of a supernatural manifestation, i.e., whether it is from God or from Satan (Acts 16:16–18). (8) Other (Tongues) Languages, a supernatural ability to speak in an unlearned language to bring a message to the church. (9) Interpretation of (tongues) languages, a supernatural ability to interpret (not translate) messages in "tongues."

These gifts are given for the profit of the body of Christ in order that they be blessed and equipped to minister the life of Christ to the world (I Corinthians 12:11–30).

The gift of "tongues" to the church is not to be confused with the "tongues" of praise received as an initial evidence of the filling of the Holy Spirit. Tongues of praise and prayer are not given for the blessing of the church gathering but to edify and bless the person speaking them (I Corinthians 14:2, 4). These kinds of tongues are practiced primarily in the prayer closet (I Corinthians 14:18, 19).

Do you teach people to seek the "unknown tongue?"
No. We teach people to believe the Word of God as it is written and to set their affections on the Lord Jesus Christ. Jesus taught His disciples to receive the promised Baptism of the Holy Spirit (Acts 1:4–5; Matthew 3:11). When they received, they spoke in unlearned languages (Acts 2:4; 10:44; 19:6).

We expect no less and receive no less than these early disciples. We have no argument with those who are satisfied with less than what the Scripture says is available. The emphasis is not on "tongues" but on praising and magnifying Jesus from the heart. We have found that the only people who have to be taught concerning speaking in tongues are those who had been taught against them. Those who have not been taught to fear the unknown tongue immediately began to speak in tongues when the Spirit of God flows out of them in rivers of praise to the Lord (John 7:38–39).

Glossalalia

Doesn't the Scripture say in I Corinthians 13:8 that "unknown tongues" shall cease?

Yes. It also says that prophecy and knowledge shall cease. Notice when they shall cease—verse 10—"When that which is perfect shall come, THEN that which is in part shall be done away." Notice also verse 12. "For now we see through a glass darkly; but **then** face to face: now I know in part; but **THEN** shall I know even as also I am known."

The key to these verses is the word **then.** When shall we see everything clearly—face to face? When shall perfection come? I believe it will be when Jesus returns and restores all things to perfection. Until **then** we see through a glass darkly. Until **then** all of us should "follow after love, and desire spiritual gifts" (I Corinthians 14:1).

Since tongues is mentioned last among the gifts in I Corinthians 12:28, doesn't this mean that it is the least of the gifts and should not be sought after?

There are two listings of gifts in I Corinthians 12. The first is in verses 8–10. Tongues and interpretations are listed last. The second list is in verse 28. Again tongues and interpretations are listed last. Many have taught that they are listed last because they are least in importance.

Even if this is so, they are listed among the gifts and, therefore, should not be despised (I Corinthians 12:18–22). To be listed last does not make it undesirable, nor does it necessarily mean that it is least because last. For example: I Corinthians 13:13 reads, "And now abideth faith, hope, love, these three; but the greatest of these is love." Love is listed last. II Peter 1:5–7 lists several virtues which Christians should strive for. Love is listed last here also. Then in I Corinthians 13 tongues are mentioned first in the list. Now I am not saying that tongues is first in value. I simply state that this argument in tongues being least because listed last falls flat if used consistently.

Paul stated in I Corinthians 14:5, "I would that ye all spake in tongues." He made his position clear throughout this chapter that "tongues" have a place in worship but not the only place. WE SHOULD STRIVE FOR THE BALANCE.

I have been told that Paul wrote only to the Corinthians about the "unknown tongue" and condemned them for speaking tongues. Is this so?

Yes and no. Paul wrote only to the Corinthians about the "unknown tongue," but he did not condemn them for speaking in tongues. He wrote only to the Corinthians about the Lord's Supper. He corrected them for their abuse of the communion time and for their abuse of "tongues" and prophecy (I Corinthians 11 and 14).

If other churches had been out of order in these activities, I am sure he would have written to correct them. One thing for sure—if we reject tongues for these reasons, we must in all honesty reject the Lord's Supper. However, we need not reject either; we must only know the difference between rejection and restraint.

It seems to me that I Corinthians 14: 1, 2, 5, 14, 15 and 18 encourage speaking in tongues. The summary in verses 39 and 40, ". . . forbid not to speak with tongues. Let all things be done decently and in order."

Speaking in tongues is not our main doctrine. Our main doctrine is Jesus Christ, crucified, resurrected, glorified, and coming again. Because of our being Baptists, we are constantly questioned about our belief in speaking in tongues.

However, the Baptism of the Holy Spirit with the evidence of speaking in tongues is for all believers of all denominations. Christians from every denomination are experiencing this phenomenon, and it is causing quite a stir around the world. Our explanation is the same as Peter's in Acts 2:16, "This is that."

Isn't tongues for the immature? Isn't this implied in I Corinthians 13:11 and I Corinthians 14:20?

I quote the Scriptures referred to: I Corinthians 13:11, "When I was a child, I spake as a child, I understood as a child, I thought as a child; but when I became a man, I put away childish things." Then I Corinthians 14:20, "Brethren, be not children in understanding: howbeit in malice be ye children but in understanding be men."

The childish things (malice, suspicion, egotism, etc.) mentioned in I Corinthians 13 were caused by a lack of love. The gifts of the Holy Spirit (I Corinthians 12:8–11) do not take the place of the fruit of the Spirit (Galatians 5:22–23). The gifts of the Spirit are just that—"gifts." They are received by faith by any believer and do not indicate maturity. The fruit of the Spirit results from walking in the Spirit. Love is imparted by the Spirit but is listed as fruit and not as a gift (Galatians 5:22). A person needs both power and love. In fact, the gifts are to be operated in love. Many who have received "gifts" need to walk in love and stop the childish immature ways manifested in the work of God. I believe both I Corinthians 13:11 and I Corinthians 14:20 are speaking to immature Christians who are doing harm with gifts by lack of wisdom and love.

In answering your questions—no, I do not believe that tongues are just for the immature. If so, Paul was immature for he said, "I speak in tongues more than you all" (I Corinthians 14:18). I do believe that we should strive for maturity in the manifestation of the gifts.

According to what you previously wrote, it is not necessary to speak in tongues to be saved and go to heaven. What is the purpose then? It is hard for me to understand the benefits of speaking something if I don't know what I am saying.

It is understandable from a natural viewpoint to question the value of "speaking in tongues." This also was a question in my mind until I was willing to accept the Word of God rather than reason the "whys" and "hows" of this phenomenon.

The Scriptures say that the early church spoke in tongues as evidence that they had been Baptized IN the Holy Spirit (Acts 2:4; 10:44-46; 19:1-6).

It is also recorded that speaking in tongues EDIFIES the believer when practiced by him in private devotions (I Corinthians 14:4; Jude 20). The word EDIFY means to construct or improve. It is derived from the Latin word AEDES which means **fireplace.** By praying in the Spirit, we can become aglow with the Spirit. That is why Paul said, "I thank my God I speak in tongues more than you all" (I Corinthians 14:18). He explained that his main speaking in tongues was not at church but in his private devotions.

There is a gift of tongues (I Corinthians 2:10) for the church gatherings which requires interpretation (I Corinthians 14:5, 13, 28). This gift plus the gift of interpretation helps the church (I Corinthians 14:5, 15).

To explain all the "hows" and "whys" of the Spirit of God is beyond my ability. I cannot even explain why singing praises in English builds our faith (Colossians 3:16). I'm glad that Jesus did not say, "Understand the Spirit" but "Receive the Spirit" (John 20:22). "Oh, the depth of the riches both of the wisdom and knowledge of God. How unsearchable are his judgments, and his ways past finding out! For who hath known the mind of the Lord? Or who hath been his counselor?" (Romans 11:33–34.)

In I Corinthians 12:30 Paul asks, "Do all speak with tongues?" The obvious answer is, "No." Can you explain your teaching that all Christians should speak in tongues?

In I Corinthians 12:29–30 Paul asks, "Are all apostles? Are all prophets? Are all teachers?" etc. Do all speak with tongues? You are right. The obvious answer is, "No." All do not have the ministry of an apostle, or the ministry to be used of God to speak messages in tongues in a service, which require interpretation (I Corinthians 14:26–28). But there was no interpretation of tongues in the house of Cornelius (Acts 10:44–48), nor at Ephesus (Acts 19:1–6). Interpretation was not necessary as all the believers were praising and worshipping God and were not speaking to men (I Corinthians 14:2). But **some** in the Church do have the ministry to speak to men "in tongues" and **some** have the ministry of interpretation (I Corinthians 14:27).

Isn't the main evidence of the fullness of the Holy Spirit the power to witness for the Lord Jesus (Acts 1–8)? Why do some believe that "tongues" is the evidence?

To answer your question I need to quote Acts 1:8—"But ye shall receive power after that the Holy Ghost is come upon you: and ye shall be witnesses unto me both in Jerusalem, and in all Judea and in Samaria, and unto the uttermost part of the earth."

Notice "ye shall be witnesses," not "ye **should** be witnesses. The early disciples were witnesses of Jesus. The emphasis is being a witness to the resurrection of Jesus Christ and not "doing witnessing." The book of Acts reveals how they witnessed. They witnessed by their supernatural works that Jesus is alive (Acts 3:1–13; 8:5–8; 14:11, etc.). They witnessed by their ways (Acts 2:46–47; 4:13). They witnessed by their words (Acts 5:41, 42; 8:4; 17:6). In other words, they performed the works of a resurrected Christ (John 14:12). They acted like Christ, and they talked about Christ. All of this witnessing was a result of their being filled with the Holy Spirit and the Spirit-filled Christian will do the same in our day.

Speaking in tongues is not an end. It is a means to an end. According to I Corinthians 14:4, "He that speaketh in an unknown tongue edifieth himself." In other words, he builds up his faith. Paul called this "Praying in the Spirit" (I Corinthians 14:15).

In Jude 20 we are told to build up ourselves in our most Holy Faith, praying in the Holy Ghost. I believe that this means we build up our faith to be witnesses for our Lord. We believe in talking for Jesus. That is why I preach thirty minutes each day by radio in the West Indies and thirty minutes each day by radio in the Philippines. That is why one-third of our budget is spent on missions. Hundreds of souls are being saved by our testimony to a resurrected Lord. To God be the glory (Psalms 105:1–2).

Why should God choose unknown tongues as the initial evidence of the Baptism in the Holy Spirit?

The Scriptures say: "O the depth of the riches both of the wisdom and knowledge of God! How unsearchable are His judgments, and His ways past finding out! For who hath known the Mind of the Lord? Or who hath been His counselor?" (Romans 11:33–34). Some things God does are some-

Glossalalia

what mysterious. However, I believe that speaking in an unknown language by the Spirit gives a person an unlimited vocabulary with which to give vent to His praises. With such a mighty force of the Holy Spirit upon the human spirit, how could he possibly remain quiet and composed? Jesus said that "out of his belly shall flow rivers of living water" (John 7:38). These rivers of praise flow out in glorious supernatural words to God who understands the language of the heart.

The tongue has tremendous power for good and evil (James 3 and Matthew 12:37). The Holy Spirit singles out this most important faculty in man as the initial physical evidence of His infilling. With the tongue we witness to men, but our first witness will be praises unto God (Acts 1:8).

Last Sunday three young people were filled with the Spirit at Liberty Baptist Church. They spoke with "tongues." On Monday a Baptist minister was filled with the Spirit in our prayer room. He spoke with tongues. I believe the question, "Do I have to speak in tongues?" should be changed to, "Do you mean I get to speak in tongues?"

How does a person feel or react when he receives the Baptism in the Holy Spirit?

I assume you are not speaking of supernatural manifestations, such as speaking in tongues, but of physical feelings. Since no two persons have the same personality traits, no two will feel or react exactly the same. Nor will the same person feel or react the same way all the time.

Some are extroverts, others are introverts; some have exuberant joy, others receive a sweet peace; but all know that something fresh from God has been given to them. The reality of any spiritual experience should not be determined just by feelings, but by faith in the Word of God. However, I feel as one brother said, "I don't go by feelings, but I'm glad that

What's Your Question?

sometimes I can feel what I'm going by." Don't seek for feelings. Seek the Holy Spirit according to Luke 11:13. He will take care of feelings.

Can I receive the Baptism of the Holy Spirit without "tongues"?

This is a point of contention with many. I can only say that the early church members spoke in tongues when they received the Baptism in the Holy Spirit (Acts 10:46; Acts 2:4; Acts 19:6). Paul spoke in tongues (I Corinthians 14:18).

We do not teach that the glossalalia (speaking in tongues) is the only evidence of the Baptism of the Holy Spirit. We do believe that God in His sovereignty has provided a way whereby we can know without doubt that we have received the enduement from on high—i.e., by speaking with other tongues as the Spirit gives utterance. We understand that this teaching has provoked much controversy in fundamental ranks of Christianity. We have been told that we should not preach that which causes so much division and strife. However, we cannot dismiss speaking in tongues as inconsequential in relation to the Baptism of the Holy Spirit. We seek not tongues for tongues' sake; we simply believe that present-day Christians have the same need as early-day Christians—a way of communicating with God by the Holy Spirit. One brother declares: "If I buy a pair of shoes and the tongue is in the shoe, I will not mention them. However, if no tongue is in the shoe, I will probably ask if something isn't missing."

If a person is satisfied without the evidence of speaking in tongues, we have no argument with him. Perhaps his sense of need is not as great as ours. However, I believe the question should not be "Do I have to speak in tongues?" but "Do I have the privilege of praising God from my spirit in another language?" (I Corinthians 14:2).

Glossalalia

I have heard that you teach that any person who has received the Baptism in the Holy Spirit can speak in tongues whenever he wants to. Is this true? I thought speaking in tongues was entirely supernatural.

Paul said: "For if **I** pray in an unknown tongue, **my spirit prayeth,** but my understanding is unfruitful. What is it then? **I will** pray in the Spirit and **I will** pray in the understanding also: **I will** sing with the spirit, and **I will** sing with the understanding also" (I Corinthians 14:14–15). Notice that Paul did not say that the Holy Spirit prays, but "my spirit prayeth." The Holy Spirit miraculously gives the words, but the person speaks by an act of his will.

There are times when the anointing for the ability to speak in tongues is greater than at other times; however, the man's will is in control at all times. The speaking is not supernatural. What is spoken is supernatural. If this is not true, how could Paul place a limit on the number who speak in tongues in a service (I Corinthians 14:27)? He adds in verse 32: "And the spirits of the prophets are subject to the prophets."

Many never exercise their freedom to pray in the Spirit because they are afraid of getting in the flesh. Dear Christian friend, obey Jude's admonition (Jude 20), "But ye beloved, building up yourselves on your most holy faith, praying in the Holy Ghost." Take a position of faith, not doubt. Expect a supernatural move upon you. Your part is to begin speaking as a result of the Spirit's moving. Rejoice to speak whatever sounds the Spirit gives. God will do His part if you believe. Do your part by praising or praying according to the prompting of the Holy Spirit. If you do this regularly, you will find your faith increasing (I Corinthians 14:4). Paul spoke in tongues more than the Corinthians in order to build himself up in the faith (I Corinthians 14:8). Why not cast

What's Your Question?

aside your doubts and confess with Paul, "I will pray in the Spirit . . ."

I desire all that Jesus wants me to receive, but doesn't a person receive the Holy Spirit when he gets saved?

Yes, a person does receive the Holy Spirit when he receives salvation. Romans 8:9, "If any man have not the Spirit of Christ, he is none of his." I Corinthians 12:3, "No man can say that Jesus is Lord but by the Holy Ghost."

If a person is saved, he is saved by the regeneration of the Holy Spirit. However, it is one thing to receive the Holy Spirit into your heart. It is another experience to be filled or controlled by the Holy Spirit (Ephesians 5:18). Every Christian needs to be filled with the Holy Spirit.

There are two words in the original language translated receive in the King James Version of the Bible. One is "Dekomai" (Acts 8:14), which means to receive something or someone into your heart. The other word is "Lambano" (Acts 8:15), which means to receive in the sense of welcome or give control to the person coming in.

The believers at Samaria had received (Dekomai) the Lord and had been baptized but later received (Lambano) the Holy Spirit (Acts 8:17).

NOTE: Liberty Baptist Church does not major on the subject of the "unknown" tongue. Seldom do we teach on the matter in our church services. Since our people magnify the Lord in other tongues, this naturally causes questions about the matter. We are happy to attempt to answer these questions, but I hope it is understood that we do not harp on the subject of tongues. We believe in the entire Bible as God's revelation to man, and we attempt to keep a balance in our teaching, majoring on the person of Jesus Christ our Lord.

Glossalalia

Dear Bro. Sumrall: I read your answers in the paper each Sunday and I think they are wonderful. In fact, I have cut each one out and filed them.

I have been filled with the Holy Spirit for many years and, praise God, it is still a fresh experience with me. It's hard for me to understand why all Christians do not desire the Baptism in the Holy Spirit with tongues. What have you found to be the greatest hindrances to people receiving the Spirit?

After considerable thought and attempts to give a brief answer to this question, I decided it might be helpful to some for me to write a series of articles to be published consecutively for several Sundays.

In the first place, there are many who simply do not know about the Baptism in the Holy Spirit. When Paul visited Ephesus for the first time, he found twelve disciples who had never heard of the Holy Spirit (Acts 19:1–6). After explaining to them the full message that John the Baptist preached (Matthew 3:11), he baptized in the Name (or by the authority) of Jesus Christ. Then he laid hands on them and they received the Holy Spirit "and they spake in tongues and prophesied."

In most every place I find believers who have never been taught about their privilege of receiving the Holy Spirit according to the Scriptures. But, praise the Lord, people from all denominations are hearing the full Gospel and are humbly, but gladly, receiving the Power of God through the Baptism in the Holy Spirit.

We will send literature to anyone desiring to know more about this supernatural phenomena. Write to: Liberty Baptist Church, P. O. Box 3138, Pensacola, Fla. 32506.

NOTE: This article is a continuation of the answer to the question: "What are the greatest hindrances to Christians receiving the Baptism in the Holy Spirit?"

What's Your Question?

Another great hindrance to receiving the Holy Spirit by all the believers is the misuse of the doctrine of "dispensationalism." The word **dispensation** in theology means a specific arrangement of the periods of time in Bible history. Mr. Scofield in his Bible notes presents seven dispensations, which are: (1) Innocence, the age from the creation of man to his fall; (2) Conscience, the age from the fall of man to the flood; (3) Human government, the age from the flood to the call of Abraham; (4) Promise, the age from Abraham to the exodus to Israel from Egypt; (5) Law, the age from the exodus to the crucifixion of Jesus Christ; (6) Grace, the age from the crucifixion to the second coming of Christ; (7) Divine Government, the age from the second coming for a period of 1,000 years.

I believe there is merit to these dispensations, but I was taught in my theological training that "tongues" and other supernatural phenomena belonged to the early Church period only. I paraphrased the Book of Acts in my undergraduate work, but I dispensationalized all the physical miracles back to another age, not realizing that we have been in the dispensation of Grace (which is another word for gift) since the crucifixion. In this age, the Holy Spirit is on earth administrating the affairs of God, convicting men of sin, regenerating them by His Power, and equipping them for service for the Lord Jesus. The present-day Church needs the works of the Holy Spirit (I Corinthians 12:8–11) as much or perhaps more than the early Church did. Praise the Lord, a host of people are learning this and are obeying the Scriptures which tell us to be filled with the Spirit and to seek for the gifts of the Holy Spirit (Ephesians 5:18; I Corinthians 12:31).

NOTE: This article is a continuation of the answer to the question: "What are the greatest hindrances to Christians receiving the Baptism in the Holy Spirit?"

Glossalalia

A third reason that God's people do not receive all that is promised to them by the Lord, which includes the Baptism in the Holy Spirit and the operation of the gifts of the Spirit, is the misuse of the gifts of the Spirit by a small percentage of those who receive the Power of God.

If you question the possibility of the misuse of the gifts, read about Balaam and Samson in the Old Testament. I Corinthians 12-14 were written to explain the gifts of the Spirit and to correct misuse of them.

We can attribute a part of the misuse of the gifts to a lack of wisdom. Then some misuse the gifts because of a lack of love (I Corinthians 13). Most of us have seen healing meetings that left us cold because of the emphasis on money. The leaders of such campaigns are as "sounding brass and tinkling cymbals (I Corinthians 13:1-3). God says in Ezekiel 34:28, "seemeth it a small thing unto you to have eaten up the good pasture, but ye must tread down with your feet the residue of your pastures? And to have drunk of the deep waters, but ye must foul the residue with your feet? And as for my flock, they eat that which ye have trodden with your feet; and they drink that which ye have fouled with your feet."

However, we must keep our eyes on the Scriptures rather than of the misfits and those who do not use wisdom in the use of the gifts of God. "Prove all things; hold fast to that which is good" (I Thessalonians 5:21). Learn to discern between "the precious and the vile" (Jeremiah 15:19).

NOTE: This article is the last in a series of answers to the question: "What are the greatest hindrances to Christians receiving the Baptism in the Holy Spirit?"

In my final article on this question, I would like to quote the words of Jesus in John 5:44, "How can ye believe, which receive honour one of another, and seek not the honour that cometh from God only?"

What's Your Question?

The desire for prestige among God's people has kept many of them from completely "selling out" to God and receiving the Baptism in the Holy Spirit along with the stigma of "other tongues." The Bible calls this "the pride of life" (I John 2:16). It could be denominational pride, social pride or intellectual pride. Pride is the father of prejudice, which rejects anything that is not incorporated in the teachings of its social or denominational group. God desires to reveal Himself to man but has "hidden these things from the wise and prudent and hast revealed them unto babes" (Luke 10:21).

It remains to be seen how far the present-day Church can go in defeating the Devil and destroying his works if it desires only the honour that comes from God. I do not mean that we do not need each other or that we should not desire one another's love. I am speaking of the difference in seeking honour from men or from God.

Those who are willing to lay aside false pride and prejudices and truly seek God will be led into all truth by the Holy Spirit who is given unto us (John 16:13). Read Jesus' promise in Luke 11:9–13.

You said in your column that "unknown tongues" is supernatural and God understands the language. Why don't you accept other supernatural powers endowed to men by God, i.e., clairvoyance . . . etc.? These powers are Holy Spirit and there are many such stories in the Bible in accord with this.

I do not doubt that clairvoyance, seances, etc., are supernatural, but I do not believe that they are of the Holy Spirit. The Scriptures are clear that all supernatural powers are not from the God of our Lord Jesus Christ. We are to try the spirits to find out from whence they come (I John 4:1). I have yet to find a person who practices clairvoyance who believes

Glossalalia

the whole Bible is God's inspired Word or who believes that man is a sinner who has to be saved by the Blood of Jesus Christ, or who believes in eternal punishment. II Thessalonians 2:8–11 reveals that Satan can work signs and lying wonders. Many are being deceived by these lying spirits. II Corinthians 4:4 tells us that the god of this world (Satan) blinds people who will not believe the truth. May God help you to shake yourself loose from these blinding spirits lest your fate be as Saul's (I Samuel 28), who attended a chairvoyance seance.

I believe that God works supernaturally, but I try all things by the whole Word of God.

There have been doubts in my mind about the reality of messages in other "tongues." Especially this is true when the interpretation in English is much longer than the message in an unknown tongue. Does it come word by word or is it given completely to the interpreter while it is being spoken, and he has to remember it? I hope I made these questions clear, as I and several others are wondering about these things. Thank you for the help you have been with your answers. I look forward to reading them each week.

Remember that interpretation and translation are not the same. Translation is word for word, and interpretation is giving the meaning of the message.

As the message in tongues is supernatural, so is the interpretation. The same kind of inspiration that brings the message in tongues brings the interpretation in tongues. Therefore, it is not a matter of remembering words.

As I have preached in several countries through interpreters, I have been made more aware of the necessity for an interpreter to use more words in the native language to explain

What's Your Question?

the meaning of the English words. This is also true in the realm of interpretation of unknown languages. The interpretation can be longer than the original message.

We have also learned that sometimes a person is praying in tongues for the church rather than giving a message to the church. What is given in English is not interpretation but an answer to the prayer by prophecy. An answer to prayer can be a short answer or a longer one. This cleared up a lot of doubts for me. I hope it will do the same for your group.

Honestly, don't you think the present-day interest in "tongues" is just a desire for something sensational? Is this just sensationalism, or is it deeper than that?

Praise God, it is exciting, but I believe as you do that many in this generation are seeking excitement for the sake of excitement. This is true for some who get involved in the Charismatic Revival. These usually drop out when the going gets rough.

However, there is nothing at all wrong with the sensational aspect in Christianity. It surely would have been sensational to follow Jesus around for three and one-half years while He healed the sick and cast out devils. Religious leaders of that day said that the followers of Jesus were too sensational (Luke 19:37–40). It would have been sensational to be a part of the early Church and witness the Holy Spirit working—the disciples casting out devils, healing the sick, teaching the Word and adding to the Church **and they spoke in tongues.** Do you ever wonder in what Church Jesus would feel most at home if He were on earth? I'm sure that it would be where the Holy Spirit works and the people praise and worship from their hearts (Acts 2:42–47).

One man recently gave testimony that he had gotten sick and tired of being sick and tired. He began to seek the Lord

Glossalalia

with all his heart and was filled with the Holy Spirit speaking in other tongues.

I have seen nominal Christians transformed into faithful, stable disciples by receiving the Baptism in the Holy Spirit with the ability to speak in other tongues. Why shouldn't this be so when the Scriptures say that one is built up in the **Faith** by speaking in tongues (I Corinthians 14:5). "The just shall live by faith" (Romans 1:17). It seems to me that many present-day Churches could stand some deliverance from the formal, drab sameness into the glorious liberty which the Spirit gives (II Corinthians 3:17).

Did you know that it is common knowledge that heathen who worship idols have been heard speaking in tongues cursing Jesus? Could it be, dear sir, that you and your followers are deluded by evil spirits into speaking in these fanatical babblings?

There may be heathen who have spoken in "tongues" by the Devil's power. **I don't know** because I have never personally heard one doing so, **have you?** Hearsay evidence will not stand in any court room; neither is it good to repeat things that cannot be documented—that is, tell where the heathen were who spoke in tongues, who interpreted their tongues, and under what circumstances did they speak.

I know that many people have been warned that they may get some supernatural manifestation from the Devil while they are seeking for the Baptism in the Holy Spirit. It may be possible for a lost person seeking for something supernatural to receive an evil spirit. However, if a person is sincerely seeking Jesus, or if he is a believer seeking for the Baptism of the Holy Spirit, Jesus tells us He will not get a counterfeit. "If a **son** shall ask bread of any of you that is a father, will he give him a stone? Or if he ask a fish, will he for a fish give him a serpent? Or if he ask an egg, will he offer him a scorpion? If ye then, being evil, know how to give good gifts unto your children, how much more shall your Heavenly Father **give the Holy Spirit** to them that ask Him?" (Luke 11:11–13).

Just because there are counterfeits in the area of the supernatural, including tongues, gives us no license to attribute all this supernatural phenomenon to Satan. It is sometimes easier to label than it is to investigate. It is also very dangerous to label as from the Devil that which could possibly be of the Holy Spirit. Jesus said that to attribute the works of the Holy Spirit to the Devil is blasphemy and would never be forgiven here or hereafter (Matthew 12:22–32; Mark 3:22–30; Luke 11:14–23). Since it is such a risk, I would be very careful not to label unless I was dead sure I was right.

I, nor "my followers," claim perfection; but we do trust, praise, and follow the Lord Jesus Christ. We believe in the forgiveness of sins through the Blood of Jesus, the present high priestly ministry of Jesus at the right hand of God, and His soon return for His redeemed. I doubt if the Devil is behind these beliefs.

In our efforts to point out the counterfeit, let us not forget that there is the genuine.

I must be honest and tell you that I get the impression from people who speak in tongues that they think they are better than those who do not. This has "turned me off" from seeking this experience.

I'm certainly sorry that you have gotten this impression, because speaking in tongues does not declare anyone to be holier than anyone else. We do not receive any gift because of our own holiness, but because we accept by faith what is offered by the Lord. It is true that we need to be cleansed before receiving the Holy Spirit fullness, but our cleansing comes also by faith in the Blood of Jesus Christ. God never gives the Holy Spirit or any gift of the Spirit as a reward for Christian Character. The Holy Spirit is given to do IN the Christian what he cannot do FOR himself. No person is worthy to receive the Holy Spirit, nor is the Spirit given to make us better than anyone else. Our final objective is to be like Jesus. The Spirit, if we yield to Him, will change us little by little to be more like Jesus (II Corinthians 3:17–18). If you are a Christian, then you have had lost people say that they are as good as you. Evidently, they think by your testimony that you think you are better than they. You do not mean to leave that impression, but you do want them to know what you have received. Sometimes in our effort to bring people into the fullness of the Spirit, we unintentionally leave the wrong impression. I hope you will forgive all our blunders, but do not shun the experience because of our blunders. The valid way to examine the experience is by the Word of God —not by turning the spotlight on those who claim the experience.

In I Corinthians 14:15 Paul speaks of praying in the Spirit and singing in the Spirit. Also, in Jude 20 we are told to pray in the Spirit. What is your interpretation of praying and singing in the Spirit?

Paul said in I Corinthians 14:14–15: "If I pray in an unknown tongue, my spirit prayeth, but my understanding is unfruitful. What is it then? I will pray with the Spirit, and I will pray with the understanding also. I will sing with the Spirit, and I will sing with the understanding also." In other words, he is saying that praying in the Spirit is praying in a language which his mind did not understand. That is also true for singing in the Spirit.

I have heard large audiences of believers singing in the Spirit. They sound like a heavenly choir.

What's Your Question?

The next logical question is: What advantage is it to pray or sing in a language which my mind does not understand? The Word of God says that God understands (I Corinthians 14:2). That is what matters most. The Word also says that our faith is built up in this manner (I Corinthians 14:4, Jude 20). Therefore, we are encouraged to practice praying in the Spirit. We are also encouraged to pray in an understandable language when in public or else interpret what we are praying (I Corinthians 14:13).

My question for you is this: Since you believe in laying on of hands, speaking in tongues, etc., yet this is definitely not Baptist doctrine, why do you continue to call yourself a Baptist minister and your church a Baptist Church? Is it not possible that you should be affiliated with the Pentecostal groups instead? Is it because you are ashamed of being called by any other name than Baptist?

Believe me, I considered joining a Pentecostal denomination after I received the Baptism in the Holy Spirit with the evidence of speaking in an unlearned language. However, since the Baptism in the Holy Spirit is not a denomination but an experience of God for every Christian (Acts 2:39), and since I had taught and had been taught that Baptists were to believe the entire Bible, I felt constrained to remain a Baptist minister. Therefore, I remain an ordained Southern Baptist minister (page 454 of Southern Baptist Annual). The Liberty Baptist Church is not associated with the Southern Baptist Convention, though the vast majority of its members are of Southern Baptist background.

Even though we are named Baptists, we believe that all Bible-believing Christians who trust the atoning Blood of Jesus Christ and are born again are one in Christ (Ephesians 4:4-6), and the name of the local church matters very little. I minister the Word to many denominations including "Pentecostal" and "Non-Pentecostal." Denominational walls are fast tumbling down. For this I say, "Hallelujah!" May the prayer of Jesus be answered—"that they all may be one" (John 17:21).

I have been reading your articles and wonder how a Baptist minister came to believe as you do. How could you call yourself a Baptist?

The name "Baptist" is supposed to classify a person as a Bible believer. Other than that I care very little whether I am called a Baptist, Methodist, Holiness, Presbyterian, Catholic or Holy-roller. I am simply a Bible believer and a member of the body of Christ.

I have received the Baptism in the Holy Spirit with the evidence of speaking in other tongues. My church teaches that this experience is not valid. Should I remain in my church or move to another which teaches as I believe?

There are several factors involved in the answer to your question. First, I would talk to my pastor and family about the matter. If your pastor is willing for you to remain in your church and IF YOU AND THE FAMILY ARE HAPPY THERE, I see no reason to change. After all, the Baptism in the Holy Spirit is not for any one denomination, but it is an experience of God for every Christian (Acts 2:39). Secondly, if your pastor is not a man of God, then if it is in accord with your family, I would get under the supervision of a God-called pastor. Thirdly, if you feel your pastor is called of God, but he is sincerely wrong on any issue or teaching, then pray for him, but for your own profit and for the profit of the church, do not cause discord among the brethren with a "preachy" spirit. Give your testimony, but do not get "put out" with those who disagree with you. Be submissive and keep a sweet spirit (Hebrews 13:7, 17; Ephesians 4:1-4). Fourthly, if you feel the need to change churches for the sake of unity and your own spiritual life, then pray fervently and God will guide you where to go. Fifthly, sometimes in order to keep peace in the family, a person cannot do as he desires. Especially is this true in the case of a wife whose husband objects to changing churches and will not consent to her attending another church. Again, it is necessary to keep sweet and submissive. God will bring individual believers into her life to nourish her faith. He will also make her a blessing where she is. If this is your case, then I repeat: Don't be preachy, but you should never be ashamed to tell of your experience. It is from Jesus and it is real (II Timothy 1:8).

Since you believe in Acts 2:4, do you also believe in Acts 2:38? Or do you believe in baptism in the trinity as stated in Matthew 28:19?

Since I believe there is no contradiction in the Word of God, I believe both verses. Jesus gave the command in Matthew 28:20 which was to extend to the end of the age, according to this verse.

Notice that Jesus did not send His disciples with a baptismal formula but with authority to baptize believers. I believe a dumb preacher could baptize a believer saying nothing. It's not what the preacher says that is important. It is what the candidate for baptism believes in his heart that really counts (Romans 10:9-10; Acts 8:36, 39).

I am a trinitarian—meaning that I believe that the Father, Son and Holy Spirit are three distinctive persons, but one God. An example is that my wife and I are one (Matthew 19:5-6), yet we are two distinctive persons. Jesus prayed that His disciples would be as one and He and the Father are One

(John 17:21). You and I can never be the same person, but according to Jesus, He desires that we be one in heart, mind and purpose as He and the Father are one.

Since Jesus has identified Himself with mankind (Philippians 2:5-11; Hebrews 2:14-17), all authority has been given to Him in heaven and earth. To baptize in the Name of Jesus is to baptize by His authority. If a policeman says, "Stop in the name of the law," he means that the law has given him authority to stop you. When I baptize in the Name of the Father, Son and Holy Ghost, I am baptizing by the authority of Jesus Christ (Matthew 28:18) because He was the One who commanded this be done. Let me repeat—what is said by the minister is not as important as the believer's faith in the Lordship of Jesus Christ.

Enclosed is a little booklet entitled "Falsities of Modern Tongues," by A. E. Ruark. Would you please read and comment?

I read the booklet two years ago. The author's warnings are the same as those I heard for years before I received the Baptism in the Holy Spirit. In essence, he says: "Those speaking in tongues have demon spirits; they withdraw from other Christians; the Corinthians (tongue talkers) were carnal; Paul scorned tongue talkers." This particular author goes further in his blasphemy than do most authors. May God have mercy upon him.

The author tells of tests that he has made according to I John 4:1. The tests have proven, says he, that the greater majority of those who speak in tongues when asked, "Is Jesus Christ come in the flesh?" will refuse to answer that question, will give an evasive answer, or say "no" in English. I wish to speak kindly, but Mr. Ruark or anyone else is welcome to make such a test of Liberty Baptist people. Too often re-

What's Your Question?

marks have been made that reflect on God's people without proper documentation. I believe I can speak without any spirit of revenge, and say that it could be that the remarks in the little booklet are Satanic rather than the speaking in tongues.

CHAPTER TEN

MIRACLES AND HEALING

I notice on your letterheads that you believe that bodily healing is in the atonement. Would you please explain this?

As Jesus bore our sins at Calvary, so He also bore our sicknesses on the cross. Matthew 8:16–17, "When the even was come, they brought unto Him (Jesus) many that were possessed with devils and He cast out the spirits with His Word and healed all that were sick: that it may be fulfilled which was spoken by Esaias the prophet saying, 'Himself took our infirmities and bare our sicknesses'." This is a direct quote from Isaiah 53:5, which is a prophetic view of the sufferings of Christ. Jesus bore our sins (I Peter 2:24), and He bore our sicknesses (Matthew 8:16–17). The (full) gospel is that Jesus provides for the whole man through the benefits of the cross. The completion of this work in any part of man will not climax until the resurrection. However, we can appropriate the "earnest" of the redemption now by faith, i.e., forgiveness of sins and healing for our bodies (Mark 2).

Those who receive must believe for the benefits. As no sinner can be saved until he believes it is God's Will to save him and until he receives by faith, so no sick person can be healed until he believes it is God's Will to heal him and until he receives the benefits by faith. Scriptures that show how Jesus healed only those who believed for healing are: Matthew 8:8; 9:2; 9:27–30; 15:28; Mark 5:34; 10:52; Luke

What's Your Question?

17:19; John 4:47–53. The early church carried on this ministry of faith (John 14:12; Acts 14:8–10). Act now on what Jesus did for you and be healed.

How do you answer those who say that the days of miracles are past?

The days of miracles are past for those who believe that they are. "According to your faith let it be unto you" (Matthew 9:29). "All things are possible to him that believeth" (Mark 9:23). "These signs shall follow them that believe . . ." (Mark 16:17).

"One article you wrote about three weeks ago about practicing religion instead of Bible Christianity was really appreciated. I know right here in Milton quite a few people, even in my own family, who are devout church goers on Sunday but leave their Christianity in the church the balance of the week. They are even taught by their ministers that other churches only practice doctrines—false, that is.

"Your article is the first I look for in Sunday papers. Our minister says there should be no antagonism between anyone's different religions and that is to me as it should be.

"So let's keep your picture with the articles in the paper."

Questions have come from many places concerning healing for our day. This week's answer is in the form of a testimony by our evangelist who is conducting revival services at Liberty Baptist Church—Brother T. W. McGraw.

I was a businessman in Biloxi, Mississippi, with over $100,000 business, owned an apartment house and had insurance to retire on when I reached sixty years of age. Then things began to happen.

My wife was given up as hopelessly incurable. My little girl was killed at a youth camp and my little boy got his neck

Miracles and Healing

broken. I suffered three nervous breakdowns, then took arthritis of the spine and cancer. I had to sleep in a chair for eight years, lived on dope for three and one-half years. The doctors said there was no medical cure for me. All they could do was give me shots to kill pain. Then I turned to God. He completely delivered me of every disease.

I lost all my business during the period of sickness. My hospital bills were great. We lost our home and were given five days to move out. Those days were dark. I promised God to live for Him and serve Him. After weeks of fasting and prayer, God began to use me in the healing of the sick. Though I had never done any church work, calls began to come from churches for my services. Since 1963, I have seen many miracles and have led over 6,000 souls to Christ. I am not an ordained preacher. I just want to do my best for Jesus since He has done so much for me.

Do you believe it is God's Will to heal all the sick?

Since this subject causes contention among good people, I do not wish to add to the tension, which is a basic cause of sickness.

Therefore, I answer the question with "charity." We teach that Jesus bore our sins on the cross, and that He bore our sicknesses on the cross (I Peter 2:24; Matthew 8:17). The condition for receiving these benefits is faith (Ephesians 2:8; Matthew 9:29; Mark 11:22-24; 16:17; Acts 14:9 and James 5:15). On this basis, we pray for the sick in almost every service at Liberty Baptist Church. Not all are healed but many are, including those with heart disease, diabetes and cancer. I wish all were healed that we pray for. I am sure that more will be when we fully yield to the Holy Spirit to allow God's Love to flow more freely among us. As long as many are being healed and God's Word seems to endorse praying for

What's Your Question?

the sick, we shall continue by God's help to minister to the needs of those who come.

If you can heal the sick, why don't you empty out the hospitals? This would certainly prove that your healing ministry is genuine.

In the first place, I don't claim to heal the sick. I simply obey the Lord and pray for them if they desire prayer and believe that Jesus heals the body in this day. Even Jesus said, "According to your faith, let it be unto you" (Matthew 9:29).

I wish I knew more about healing the sick, but as long as some are being healed through the laying on of hands and prayer of faith, I believe it is worthwhile to continue the healing ministry. Many testimonies are available from those who have been healed at Liberty Baptist Church of deafness, heart disease, cancer, and many other diseases.

CONSIDER THIS POEM:

> "If you had been living when Christ was on earth
> And had met the Saviour kind,
> What would you have asked Him to do for you,
> Supposing that you were stone blind?"

> The child considered, and then replied,
> "I expect that without doubt,
> I'd have asked for a dog with collar and chain,
> To lead me daily about."

> And how often thus, in our faithless prayers,
> We acknowledge with shamed surprise,
> We have only asked for a dog and chain,
> When we might have had opened eyes!

Miracles and Healing

Would you please explain James 5:14–15? Was the oil medicine? If not, what good would it do to place oil on a person?

I quote the verses: "Is any sick among you? Let him call for the elders of the church; and let them pray over him, anointing him with oil in the Name of the Lord. And the prayer of faith shall save (deliver) the sick, and the Lord shall raise him up; and if he have committed sins, they shall be forgiven him."

Please note that they were to call the elders first, not the doctor. We believe in the ministry of doctors. In fact, three wonderful doctors were in Liberty Baptist Church to testify during the last two weeks. These men are surgeons who by the knowledge of medical science help hundreds; but they also believe that God can heal believers without their help, and they pray for the sick and witness miracles. I say this that you may know that we believe in the use of doctors. However, there is no mention of doctors in the above verses; but elders, who are the overseers of the flock of God (Acts 20:17, 28), were told to anoint with oil which is a symbol of the Holy Spirit. But it is not the oil that heals the sick but the prayer of faith. The oil is used as a point of contact to help release faith. The disciples used oil for this purpose during the earthly ministry of Jesus (Mark 6:12–13). We often use oil to anoint the sick at their request. I don't claim to understand all the "why." We simply obey the Scriptures and God heals the sick.

I have heard ministers talk about prayer cloths. What do they mean?

The "prayer cloth" is taken from Acts 19:12 which states: "And God wrought special miracles by the hand of Paul: so that from his body were brought unto the sick handkerchiefs or aprons, and the diseases departed from them, and the evil spirits went out of them."

This means of bringing deliverance has been used very effectively with many "Full Gospel" groups, including the Liberty Baptist Church. However, it was not intended that this method be used as "magic" or as a gimmick to get "radio offerings." I will not explain this statement in detail, but suffice it to say that some have brought "prayer cloths" into reproach by their unwise use of them, and sometimes by their obvious covetous intentions.

However, in spite of all the "quacks" who use this method, it is Scriptural. Let us remember that even the Bible has had gross misuse (II Corinthians 3:17; 4:2).

Many can testify that prayer cloths have worked for them. If you are asking how this simple method can bring healing, I can only answer I do not know all the answers. There could be a transfer of power through the cloth; but personally, I think the prayer cloth is a tangible way to release faith in the one needing help and in the ones who send it. "The prayer of faith shall deliver the sick" (James 5:15).

CHAPTER ELEVEN
RACIAL ISSUES

What is your stand, or maybe I should ask, what is your church's stand on integration and segregation of the races?

This is not the first time I have been asked to discuss this subject in this column. I have hesitated to answer questions of this nature because the problems of racial unity are so complex and involved in our day that I would be presumptuous to declare that I have the complete answers.

We do not preach segregation or integration at Liberty Baptist Church. We do not preach nor practice violence, demonstrations, marches, etc., to obtain social "rights" for anyone. We do not believe in white power or black power; but we believe in the power of the Holy Spirit. We simply preach Christ to everyone and anyone who attends regardless of race or color.

The Scriptures give us certain basic principles which, if heeded, will help alleviate racial tensions. (1) "Do unto others as you would have them do unto you" (Matthew 7:12). (2) "If it be possible, as much as lieth within you, live peaceably with all men. Avenge not yourselves, but rather give place unto wrath; for it is written, vengeance is Mine; I will repay saith the Lord" (Romans 12:18–19). (3) Withdraw thyself from those who believe material gain is godliness and who promote discord and violence with disputings and railings (I Timothy 6:2–10; Proverbs 1:10–19). (4) Have a high

What's Your Question?

regard for law and authority and pray for men who are in places of authority (Romans 13:1-8; I Timothy 2:1-4). (5) Attempt to overcome all prejudices against another race or class of people. Peter had to overcome racial prejudice after he was converted, filled with the Holy Spirit, and was used of God mightily to preach, heal the sick, and even raise the dead (Acts 10:9-35). I am a native of Mississippi, but was never taught prejudice toward the colored race (I have had other prejudices to overcome). (6) Do not expect men who do not continually pray to solve today's problems, nor should you expect complete justice in a world controlled by the spirit of selfishness, greed, and desire for prestige. Jesus didn't receive justice either. When Christ returns, He will set things in order and set up His Kingdom of equity and justice (Isaiah 11:1-10; Isaiah 42; Revelation 20). (7) Seek not great things for yourself. The happy people are those who lose themselves serving Christ and others (Mark 8:35).

I have written to you twice concerning――――and you have not given an answer. Are you afraid to answer?

I cannot answer in the News Journal all the questions that come to me. In your particular case, I felt the question would tend to create racial tension and God knows there is already too much of that. Since you did not include your name and address, I could not send you a personal answer. If you desire an answer, send your name and address.

This question and answer column is not for debate. The Lord did not call me to be a lawyer but a witness. If you have disagreed with my answers, let's try to be pleasant about our differences.

CHAPTER TWELVE

SEX AND THE BIBLE

What does the Bible say about birth control and abortion? Are they wrong?

Birth control and abortion cannot be judged by the same principle. In birth control, or conception control, there is no destruction of life. Since **God made us to be creatures of choice and not chance,** there is no violation of Bible principle to prevent conception during the act of marital sexual intercourse.

The Bible does not teach that sexual intercourse is solely for the bearing of children. The Scriptures say: ". . . **to avoid fornication,** let every man have his own wife, and let every woman have her own husband" (I Corinthians 7:2). Neither does the Bible teach that it is sinful to waste seed. The fact is, there is enough seed in one drop of seminal fluid to populate China and India. The female ovum chooses only one of these millions of seeds during conception. All other seeds are wasted. However, abortion cannot be defended with the Scriptures since abortion is the destruction of life, or in plain words, **it is murder!** It has been proven that all a person is or ever will be is present at the instant of his conception—sex, I.Q., complexion, color of eyes, etc. Therefore, it is **then** that the soul comes into being. To deliberately destroy that life is wrong.

While birth control, in some instances, may be selfish, it is not forbidden by the Scriptures. But abortion should be defined as the killing of life already in existence.

I notice in the papers that there are ten million homosexuals in the United States. Do you believe that homosexuality is a sin?

There is a tendency to condone and excuse homosexuality in our society, but for Christians it is not a matter of what is accepted by society but what the Bible says about this practice. Because of the filthiness of homosexuality, the person practicing it is called a "dog" in the Scriptures (Deuteronomy 23:17).

It is referred to many times as unclean and unnatural (Romans 1:24, 26–27). For this sin God gives up a person or a group of persons (Romans 1:24, 26, 28). When this sin is prevalent, so is violence, self-will, hatred of authority, blasphemy and other vices (II Peter 2:10–13). This, no doubt, explains much of the violence in our country. For this reason judgment came upon Sodom and Gomorrah (Genesis 19; II Peter 2) and will come upon the U.S.A. unless we join God's side of the issue (Luke 13:1–3). The Bible tells us in I Corinthians 6:9 that the effeminate shall not inherit the Kingdom of God and in Revelation 22:15 that "dogs" will not be in heaven.

The only hope and cure for homosexuals is to be delivered by Jesus Christ and washed in His Blood (I Corinthians 6:11).

We are hearing much these days about sex education, especially about the organization called SIECUS. Does the Bible say anything about sex education for children?

Indirectly the Bible says much about sex education. The parents are to teach their children the Word of God which has much to say on the subject of MORALITY which includes the right use of sex (Deuteronomy 6:4–9; Exodus 20:14, 17; Proverbs 5:6, 7; I Corinthians 7; Hebrews 13:4; and many other Scriptures).

The parent is to use good judgment as to the readiness of a child to receive sex information. Along with sex information, the child must be taught responsibility to God and his fellow man. He is to be taught "the fear of God" and the fear of disobedience to God.

Personally, I do not want anyone teaching my child on the subject of sex unless that person has a respect for Bible morals. SIECUS (Sex Information and Educational Council of the United States) claims to be interested in morals, but an investigation of its officers will prove differently. The second vice president is the editor of "Sexology," a pornographic publication which makes no apologies for advocating premarital and extra-marital sex relations. Several other officers of SIECUS are on the board of "Sexology." Dr. Mary Calderone, executive director of SIECUS, has said, "The old 'Thou shalt nots' apply no more," and "You must determine whether to have pre-marital sex."

Many parents, who are not radicals, are making their voices heard against sex education in the schools. This is a healthy sign. May God bless our efforts to save our children from the "new morality."

Knowledge of sex without fear of God is already having its toll in unwed mothers and fathers, venereal diseases, and violence. I believe the answer is not more sexual knowledge, but a holy respect for the moral values taught in the Scriptures. Since Bible teaching has been outlawed from our schools, sex education should also be left to the parents. If parents need the know-how to teach their children, perhaps the churches should begin teaching parents on this subject.

What's Your Question?

Whenever I attempt to show my son the sin of reading "sex" magazines, he keeps telling me that the Bible is full of sex stories. What shall I tell him?

The way a story is told can make it either clean or vile. Ask your son to compare what the Bible relates about sex experiences with some of the "trash" he has read from our newsstands. No doubt, if he is honest, he will observe that the Bible never gives the details of the sex experience. On the contrary, the "sex" magazines obviously make a deliberate attempt to arouse lust in the reader by describing in detail the feelings and actions of the characters involved in the sex act. One of the purposes of the Bible is to expose sin and its terrible consequences. The writers of the "sex" magazines and producers of pornographic films obviously take pleasure in making a joke of sin.

Personally, I feel very deeply about the problems of pornography and indecent literature in our community. A person usually becomes what he thinks. Therefore, it is very important that a person's mind be upon pure things (Philippians 4:8). God will surely hold the author, the seller, and the readers of indecent literature responsible for the results. If I were owner of a store that sold these books, or owner of a movie theater that showed indecent films, I would clean house now, even if it meant losing money. It would be better to declare bankruptcy than be held responsible for placing a stumblingblock in the way of others (Matthew 18:6–9).

The Scriptures declare: "God is angry with the wicked every day" (Psa. 7:11). In my opinion, these include the pornographic literature and theater owners, viewers, and sellers.

As for your son, place good and interesting literature in your home for your son. Try to keep him so busy in healthy fun and spiritual things that he will lose his desire for the sordid and base things. I shall join you and hundreds of other concerned mothers in prayer to bind in the name of Jesus the evil spirits which are intent on destroying the souls and bodies of our youth.

CHAPTER THIRTEEN
"WORLDLY" ISSUES

What do you think about dancing? Is it a sin?

Dancing is an expression of joy and is nowhere condemned by the Scriptures. We have the record of Miriam and the women with her dancing because of their deliverance from the Egyptians (Exodus 15:20). David danced before the Ark of the Lord (I Chronicles 15:25-29), and God was pleased with David's expression of joy.

However, mixed dancing, that is, the dancing of men with women in the modern way of dancing, is wrong because it permits familiarity between the sexes which is forbidden in the Scriptures (I Peter 3:11; II Timothy 2:22, and many others).

Modern dancing to the tune of sensual music is unwholesome and has proven to have an evil effect on many who participate. No doubt there are many women who can engage in the modern dance without having evil thoughts. However, the majority of men who dance with these women, and probably all of the normal ones, do have evil thoughts.

The Scripture says, "Make no provision for the flesh to fulfill the desires thereof" (Romans 13:14). I believe the modern dance makes provision for the flesh; therefore, I advise nonparticipation for Christians.

Do you believe it is wrong to wear jewelry such as rings and

What's Your Question?

beads? Also, please tell me what you think of ladies wearing makeup.

I believe every Christian should make up his own mind about these things, and that we should not judge one another in these matters. The Scriptures used to condemn the wearing of jewelry and makeup are I Timothy 2:9-10 and I Peter 3:3-4. Please notice that these Scriptures are positive and not negative. I believe that these Scriptures teach modesty and inward adorning. I am glad that Christianity is not a matter of jewelry and makeup, but it is in the heart. Certainly every Christian should look neat and nice for his Lord and not dress to call attention to himself. But notice that the prodigal's father put a ring on his son (Luke 15:22).

We do not make an issue of jewelry and makeup at Liberty Baptist Church. Whatever a Christian does, let him do it in faith (Romans 14:22-23). And let him do it as to the Lord (Colossians 3:17, 23).

Do you think it is wrong for women to wear wigs? Isn't this a type of vanity?

I suppose many things could be vain if the motive is wrong. There was a time when men's ties were considered vain.

Personally, I do not see anything wrong with a woman wearing a wig if it doesn't make her look conspicuous and different from her usual looks.

In fact, if the Scriptures give a viewpoint, it would be in favor since wigs provide a covering (I Corinthians 11). I am told that wigs also save trips to the beauty parlors and, therefore, save time and money. Frankly, I think there are many more important things to preach about than wigs, etc. All of us should make sure that we do not identify ourselves with the world or create lust by our dress or undress. Beyond that, look as nice as you can and let others do the same.

If you have enjoyed this book, you will want to read other inexpensive publications published and distributed by WHITAKER BOOKS.

Over 300 other books and cassettes are available to accommodate your needs. Two of these books are advertised on the next page of this book. They are bestsellers. To order these or any of our publications, please mail the coupon below. Good quantity discounts will be shown in the catalog.

------------------------- DETACH HERE -------------------------

WHITAKER BOOKS
504 Laurel Drive
Monroeville, Penna. 15146
Phone: 412 372–6420

Please send me a free catalog on your publications:

Name_____

Address_____

_____ Zip Code_____

Two Outstanding Books!

FACE UP WITH A MIRACLE
By Don Basham

Yes, this is a fascinating book about God, the Holy Spirit bringing new dimension to the lives of twentieth-century Christians. It is filled with experiences that testifies to a God of miracles being unleashed in our lives RIGHT NOW.

75c

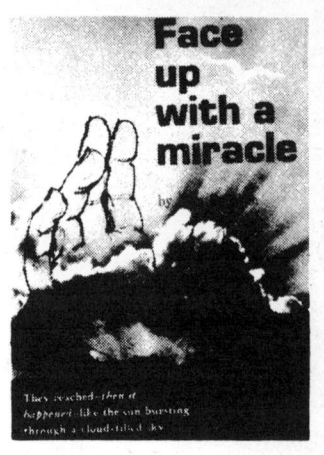

A HANDBOOK ON HOLY SPIRIT BAPTISM By Don Basham

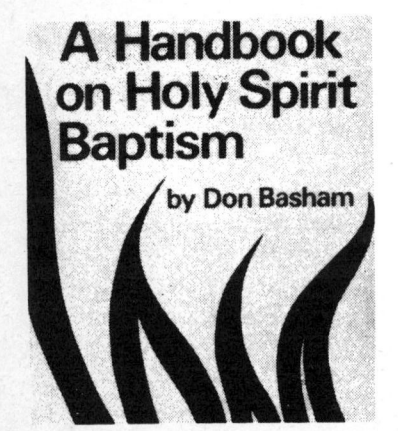

Questions and Answers on the Baptism in the Holy Spirit and speaking in tongues. A book that is in great demand which answers many important questions in Ecumenical Circles and in the Contemporary Christian Church.

$1.00